THE HALIFAX EXPLOSION

THE HALIFAX EXPLOSION

Surviving the Blast that Shook a Nation

HISTORY/HUMAN INTEREST

Joyce Glasner

PUBLISHED BY ALTITUDE PUBLISHING CANADA LTD.
1500 Railway Avenue, Canmore, Alberta T1W 1P6
www.altitudepublishing.com
1-800-957-6888

Extreme care has been taken to ensure that all information presented in
this book is accurate and up to date. Neither the author nor the
publisher can be held responsible for any errors.

Publisher	Stephen Hutchings
Associate Publisher	Kara Turner
Project Editor	Jill Foran
Editor	Jennifer Nault
Digital Photo Colouring	Scott Manktelow

We acknowledge the financial support of the Government
of Canada through the Book Publishing Industry Development
Program (BPIDP) for our publishing activities.

Altitude GreenTree Program
Altitude Publishing will plant twice as many trees as were used
in the manufacturing of this product.

National Library of Canada Cataloguing in Publication Data

Glasner, Joyce
The Halifax explosion / Joyce Glasner.

(Amazing stories)
Includes bibliographical references.
ISBN 1-55153-942-X

1. Halifax (N.S.)--History--Explosion, 1917. I. Title. II. Series:
Amazing stories (Canmore, Alta.)

FC2346.4.G53 2003   971.6'22503   C2003-905480-2

An application for the trademark for Amazing Stories™
has been made and the registered trademark is pending.

Printed and bound in Canada by Friesens
2 4 6 8 9 7 5 3

Cover: A view across Halifax Harbour after the blast

For my husband, Doug

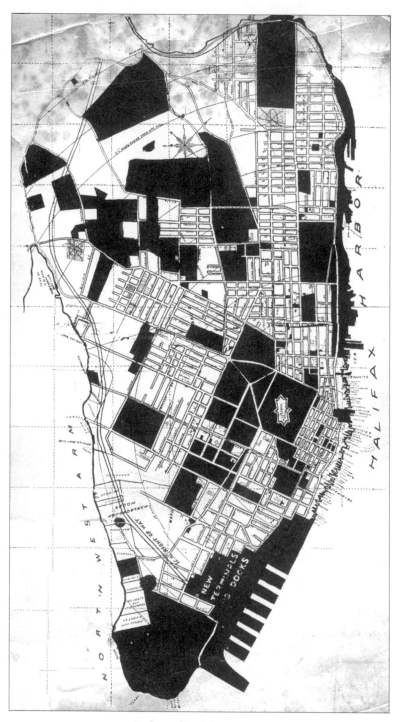

A plan of Halifax c. 1910

Contents

Prologue

Billy Wells jammed the gas pedal to the floor and squeezed the horn as they flew by a team of Clydesdales pulling a wagon loaded with barrels. Driving "Patricia," the station's new motorized fire truck, at top speed through the city was the most thrilling experience of the 20-year-old firefighter's life.

"Take it easy Billy!" Chief Cordon shouted, his words barely audible over the clanging bells and roaring engine.

The column of black smoke billowing high above the harbour looked ominous. Billy had never seen anything quite like it. He couldn't imagine the inferno that would produce that amount of smoke.

They arrived at the wharf to see a blazing freighter butted up against Pier 6. Multicoloured flames shot from the ship's deck high into the sky. Fire had spilled from its bow down onto the wharf, igniting the surrounding buildings. The heat from the blaze was so intense that the men had to shield their faces. Just as the firefighters on the back leaped from the truck and began unrolling the hose, the earth shuddered violently. Billy felt himself being ripped from the driver's seat and catapulted through the air. The next thing he knew, he was "quite a distance from the fire engine." Before he had a chance to move, he was swept up in a massive tidal wave. The tremendous force of the wave drove him along for hundreds of metres before slamming him against a telephone pole.

When the water receded, Billy lay in a heap at the foot of the pole. Shrapnel began raining down around him, and a greasy black substance began falling from the sky. When it was all over, he struggled to his feet and looked around in disbelief. He was halfway up the hill of Fort Needham, on the opposite side of the street from the wharf. He felt a throbbing pain in his right arm and looked down to discover Patricia's steering wheel gripped in his right hand. In a daze, he staggered through the wreckage back to Pier 6. The fire truck was upside down, several metres from where it had been parked. The shiny new vehicle was now nothing more than a twisted piece of junk. Scattered around the wreck were a few of the lifeless bodies of his fellow firefighters; the rest were nowhere in sight.

Chapter 1
At the Mouth of the Harbour

 slender crescent moon hung in the clear night sky. Its silvery light reflected faintly off the black waters of Halifax Harbour. Every five seconds, the penetrating light from the McNabs Island lighthouse beamed across the dark waters, illuminating the bow of the drab grey freighter anchored just off shore.

12:00 a.m. December 6, 1917
Unable to sleep, Captain Aimé Le Medec paced back and forth on the deck. After a harrowing five-day journey from New York, the *Mont Blanc* had arrived at the mouth of the harbour late that afternoon. Too late, Le

Medec had been informed, to enter the harbour that day.

In all his 22 years at sea, Le Medec could not remember a more stressful voyage than the one from New York to Halifax. But the Atlantic crossing — yet to come — would be far worse. The German-sub-infested waters of the Atlantic were treacherous enough for the swiftest of vessels. The British Navy had lost hundreds of ships in battles with German U-boats over the past few months. And loaded down as she was, the old French freighter could barely manage seven knots for any distance. The chances of the *Mont Blanc* keeping up with any convoy at that speed were highly improbable.

The *Mont Blanc* was a 3121-ton freighter. The merchant ship was owned and operated by the French shipping company, Compagnie Générale Transatlantic. However, she was currently under French naval orders. In ordinary circumstances, the battered, 18-year-old freighter would never have been considered for such a mission. But these days, every available vessel, no matter how dilapidated, was pressed into service for the war effort.

Prior to their arrival in New York, Le Medec had not been informed of the nature of the cargo they were to transport back to France. Therefore, it came as a shock when the stevedores began loading the hold with 2300 tons of picric acid, 200 tons of TNT, 10 tons of gun

cotton, and 35 tons of benzol. Although he'd had no previous experience with explosives, Le Medec knew this
was enough lethal material to blow the *Mont Blanc* —
and anything within range — to smithereens.

Precautions had been taken to ensure the volatile
cargo was safely stowed in the hold, and the drums of
benzol were snugly strapped on deck, away from the
other materials. Nevertheless, the thought of sailing
across the Atlantic on a floating bomb was unsettling.
The situation was aggravated when the convoy they
were to sail with from New York to Bordeaux refused to
take them along. Le Medec was informed that the
freighter would have to sail up the coast to Halifax on its
own. There, he was told, they might be accepted into a
larger convoy — one equipped with a cruiser for added
protection. But the sluggishness of the *Mont Blanc* and
her deadly cargo made her a liability. Le Medec realized
there was a distinct possibility no convoy would accept
them. In that case, he would be faced with the unthink-
able prospect of running the gauntlet alone.

Aimé Le Medec had served with Générale
Transatlantic for just over a decade, beginning as a second officer and finally achieving the rank of captain in
1916. His employers regarded the serious, 38-year-old as
capable and conscientious. Le Medec had only assumed
command of the *Mont Blanc* shortly before they set sail

from Bordeaux in November. But by the time they reached Halifax, he had already gained the respect of his 41 crewmembers.

Harbour pilot Francis Mackey boarded the *Mont Blanc* when it arrived at the examination anchorage off McNabs Island, at the mouth of Halifax Harbour. Mackey would guide the freighter into the harbour. When he came aboard late Wednesday afternoon, the pilot had some bad news for Le Medec. The anti-submarine net, a string of mines that was stretched across the harbour entrance every evening to prevent enemy vessels from entering, was already in place. They would have to spend the night anchored off McNabs Island. Anxious to get into the harbour as early as possible, Le Medec asked Mackey to stay aboard that night. The captain planned to proceed as soon as the boom opened at dawn.

Its size, shape, and location made Halifax Harbour a perfect military and naval stronghold. The city of Halifax sits on a large peninsula jutting out into the harbour, narrowing the channel between the Dartmouth shore and Halifax waterfront. The south end of the peninsula overlooks McNabs Island, and beyond that, the open waters of the Atlantic Ocean. The north end of the peninsula faces an almost completely enclosed body of water called the Bedford Basin. This configuration meant the harbour was easy to secure, making

Halifax an ideal allied port during the war. By 1917, the third year of World War I, the harbour teemed with allied cruisers, freighters, and merchant ships. The sparkling waters of the Bedford Basin were always peppered with vessels awaiting convoy.

In times of peace, Halifax was a small, sedate city with a population of about 50,000. Being a garrison town, however, meant a huge influx of military personnel swelled the population by thousands during the war. Halifax was also a city sharply divided by class distinctions. Citadel Hill was the dividing line between north and south, rich and poor. South End Halifax harboured the upper classes. Elegant tree-lined avenues and ornate Victorian mansions spread across the south end of the peninsula from Citadel Hill to Point Pleasant Park. The North End was home to the working class. This area was heavily industrialized, with factories, such as Dominion Textiles, the Acadia Sugar Refinery, and the Hillis Iron Foundry, scattered throughout. Richmond, the community that clung to the steep eastern slope of Fort Needham, was the heart of the North End. Its dirt streets and ash-strewn sidewalks were lined with the unassuming wooden homes of the men and women who worked in the area's dockyards and factories.

To Captain Aimé Le Medec, Halifax was just another port city, nothing more than a safe haven in dangerous times. That night, the city was almost invisible from where he stood. In the vast sea of darkness, the only signs of civilization were a few faint lights twinkling off in the distance.

Chapter 2
Port City Morning

t 7:30 a.m., Vincent Coleman stepped outside and took a deep breath. The early morning air was pleasantly crisp, and a light frost dusted the rooftops. Catching a whiff of briny ocean scent, he looked down Russell Street toward the harbour. A gauzy mist hovered over the glassy water. Along Barrington Street, trucks, cars, horse-drawn carts, and pedestrians moved in a steady stream as workers made their way to the factories and dockyards along the waterfront.

At 43 years of age, Vincent was a personable, well-built man of medium height and weight. A train dispatcher with the Canadian Government Railway, he was

Vincent Coleman

known to be hardworking and dependable. That December morning, Vincent felt optimistic about his life. Things finally seemed to be falling into place for him. He, his wife Frances, and their four children — Nita, Gerald, Eleanor, and Aileen (nicknamed "Babe") — had recently moved into their own home, a large new

Frances Coleman

house on the corner of Russell and Albert. It had taken years of scrimping and saving while living with relatives for the couple to save enough money to buy their own house. But in the end, it had all been worthwhile. Vincent relished the feeling of coming home in the evening; Frances and the children were thrilled to have a place they could call their own.

The past few years had been a struggle for the Colemans. Their two sons, Gerald and Cyril, had contracted diphtheria the year before. The boys were quarantined in one room of the house during their illness. Frances nursed them night and day, carefully changing her clothes and washing herself before going near the rest of the family. She was particularly concerned for Babe, who was just five months old at the time. Gerald, the older of the two boys, miraculously survived the deadly disease. However, his eight-year-old brother Cyril did not. Losing their youngest son was the most devastating thing the couple had ever faced. But Frances was a spirited woman, with extraordinary strength and resilience. Throughout the terrible ordeal, she managed to keep the family going. Moving into the new house seemed like a fresh start for the Colemans, a chance to leave the bad times behind.

Vincent sauntered down Albert Street toward his office in the railway yards. His thoughts turned to the upcoming union meeting and the badly needed wage increases the union was demanding. Christmas was just around the corner, and Vincent wanted to get Frances something nice this year.

Just as Vincent left for work, the rest of the family began to stir. While the children ate breakfast, Frances rushed around getting their clothes pressed and laid out for them. Nita, the Colemans' oldest daughter, would be staying home that morning, as she had come down with strep throat. Gerald didn't have classes until that afternoon. However, he was serving as an altar boy at morning mass at St Joseph's Church.

Across town, Jean Forrest and her parents were in the midst of breakfast when the plumbers that had been hired to fix some leaking pipes arrived at the door. Jean was annoyed that the men had arrived so early. She had a busy day ahead at the Red Cross Hospital; she disliked having her morning routine disrupted. Still, she tried her best to ignore the interruption, and continued to prepare for work.

North Street Station was bustling that morning. Men in uniform shouldering duffle bags crowded the cavernous stone building. Commuters from the outskirts of the city scurried to work, adding to the commotion. For Evelyn Fox, all the hustle and bustle seemed terribly exciting and cosmopolitan. A budding author of 15 years of age, Evelyn had just moved to the suburbs from a small coastal community. Most mornings since the school year had begun, she travelled from Bedford aboard the 8:20 Milk Train. But that morning, she was up earlier than usual and decided to travel with her father on the 7:30 Suburban. Evelyn attended the

Halifax County Academy. It was a large brick building at the foot of Citadel Hill on Brunswick Street. Her father, Arthur Fox, was principal of Alexandra School. After leaving the station, father and daughter walked in companionable silence up North Street to Brunswick, where they exchanged goodbyes and went their separate ways.

That morning, like most others, Dean John Llwyd was up early. He always tried to squeeze in an hour or two of uninterrupted writing before his ministerial duties began. In the five years that he had lived in Halifax, John Plummer Derwent Llwyd had risen from the position of Rector of All Saints Cathedral to Dean of Nova Scotia. Still, his new position had not affected his genial, caring nature or his enthusiastic interest in others. In addition to being a dean, Llwyd was also a noted author of poetry, magazine articles, and theological essays. Along with his other duties, being a devoted husband and father of three grown children left him little time to spend on his writing. These quiet morning hours were precious.

Chapter 3
A Fateful Error

The sun had not yet risen above the horizon when Le Medec was informed the *Mont Blanc* could enter the harbour. He breathed a sigh of relief as they crept toward the outer boom. Earlier, he had tried to hide his impatience while an American freighter had passed through ahead of them. Now, there was no disguising his relief from the pilot, Francis Mackey, and his first officer, who flanked him on the bridge. Although Mackey spoke no French, and Le Medec knew little English, they managed to communicate without too much difficulty. Mackey's straightforward manner impressed the French captain. He felt confident with the burly Nova Scotian guiding his ship into the harbour. Mackey had been guiding vessels in and out of Halifax Harbour for a quarter of a century without incident. He knew the harbour better than his own backyard. Every inlet, jut of shoreline, shoal, and shallow were ingrained in his memory. As this was Le Medec's first time in Halifax, he found the pilot's familiarity with the harbour reassuring. It was a clear, fine morning; visibility was good and there did not appear to be any unusual currents or conditions. As they slipped through the outer boom, Le Medec began to relax for the first time since leaving New York.

Traffic in the harbour was particularly heavy that morning. Every pier swarmed with stevedores loading and unloading shipments of lumber, food, and horses. Cruisers sat at anchor awaiting convoy. Freighters were lined up for berths.

At 8:15, Captain Horatio Brannen and his crew set out from the dry docks towing two scows of ashes. Brannen's ship, the tug SS *Stella Maris*, was under charter by the Royal Canadian Navy (RCN). Their orders that morning were to haul the ashes into the Bedford Basin and dump them. This was a routine job for Brannen and his crew, and the skipper didn't foresee any problems. However, just as they started crossing the harbour, Brannen noticed a ship steaming through the Narrows, heading straight toward them. With the unwieldy scows in tow, the captain knew he couldn't make it to the opposite side of the channel in time to avoid a collision. He decided to swing his vessel back to the Halifax side. As the steamer sailed by, he noted the name *Imo* on the bow and the words "BELGIAN RELIEF" in large, red letters on the side of her hull.

The *Imo*, a 5041-ton Norwegian tramp steamer, was chartered by the Belgian Relief Commission to transport supplies from North America to the war-torn nation of Belgium. The tramp steamer should have been halfway down the eastern seaboard by this time, but it had spent the previous day anchored in the Bedford Basin awaiting a coal shipment. Unfortunately, the shipment had been late arriving. By the time the coal was finally loaded, the anti-submarine net was already in place. As a result, they were forced to spend an extra night in port. Captain Haakon From was furious about the delay. Anxious to proceed to New York where they were to pick up a load of grain, Captain From suggested pilot William Hays speed up their passage through the harbour. Hays complied. He pushed the steamer two knots over the harbour's speed limit of five knots, despite the fact that the helm was sluggish and unresponsive.

As the *Imo* sped through the Narrows it confronted the same American freighter that had sailed through the boom ahead of the *Mont Blanc.* The freighter, heading into the Bedford Basin, was too far into the *Imo*'s water to corr⌐ct her course. So, rather than passing each other in the conventional port-to-port manner, the skipper of the American ship signalled that he was maintaining course to the left. The *Imo* acknowledged the signal, and the two ships steamed by one another. Fortunately, they passed without incident. After passing the American freighter, the *Imo* continued along on the same course, maintaining its speed.

Watching this close call, Captain Brannen knew his decision to sving the *Stella Maris* back toward Halifax had been wise. Brannen, his first mate (and son), Walter Brannen, and William Knickerson stood on the bridge of their vessel, keeping a close watch on the *Imo* as it barrelled through the busy harbour. All three had an ominous feeling about the ship's relentless pace. Suddenly, a grey freighter appeared, heading toward them from the opposite direction. From Brannen's perspective, it was clear that the *Imo* was too far into what should have been the French ship's path.

The *Mont Blanc* gave one short whistle blast to indicate it was altering course to starboard. Astonishingly, the *Imo* responded with two blasts, signalling its intention to alter its course to port. This shift in direction would put the *Imo* even deeper into the French freighter's water. As the two ships tried to manoeuvre around one another, a flurry of whistle blasts rang out across the placid water. The *Imo* was bearing down fast on the French freighter. Brannen could see that something was terribly wrong. His pulse quickened. Unless a miracle occurred, a collision between the two ships seemed inevitable. Just then, the *Mont Blanc's* bow swung hard to port. "They're going to collide!" Knickerson shouted. Brannen gripped the deck rail and stared in disbelief as the *Imo* continued moving toward the French ship. Time seemed to slow down. The gap closed between the two ships. Then suddenly, the *Imo's* bow slammed into the *Mont Blanc's* starboard bow.

For Captain Aimé Le Medec, the moment of impact was devastating. As he watched the Norwegian ship's bow cut a three-metre gash into their starboard bow, he felt as though he had fallen into a nightmare. Physically and mentally shaken, he quickly pulled himself together and ordered the engines reversed. Captain From did the same. As the *Imo's* bow withdrew from the gash, the grinding of metal on metal created a welder's torch spray of sparks, which showered across the deck of the French freighter. Several drums of the benzol stowed on deck jerked free from their lashings and began to leak. The benzol proved to be a perfect accelerant. Once the sparks hit the benzol it was a matter of minutes before the *Mont Blanc's* deck was completely engulfed in flames. Clouds of black smoke billowed higher and higher as the fire intensified. One by one, the drums of benzol began to explode, adding more fuel to the fire.

As Le Medec struggled to remain calm and think of a viable method of fighting the blaze, his crew began to panic. The crew had spent days aboard this ship, with strict instructions not to smoke or carry matches due to the extreme fire hazard. They were all too aware of the danger they were in. Le Medec knew that his only real option was to sink the ship before it blew. Time, however, was a critical factor. A dense layer of rust welded the bolts of the seacock to the hull. In the time it would take to yank the rusted bolts, open the valve, and flood the compartments, the powder keg they were standing on would surely have exploded. All aboard would be killed. Le Medec realized his only option was to try to save his crew. By the time he finally gave the order to abandon ship, the men, fearing for their lives, had already lowered the two lifeboats into the water. The instant the order was given, they scurried down ladders and ropes, anxious to get as far from the vessel as they could before she blew.

Once the first officer was sure all hands were in the lifeboats, he reported to the captain, telling him it was time to leave. Le Medec, however, had no intention of abandoning ship. It was a captain's duty, he believed, to go down with his ship. Le Medec told his first officer that he was staying aboard and held his ground. Realizing that there was no time to argue the point, the first officer grabbed his captain and forced him down the ladder into the waiting lifeboat.

Chapter 4
The Red Flag

The sight of the burning ship in the harbour brought all activity onshore to a halt. Dockworkers dropped what they were doing and gathered in groups along the wharves to watch the action. Factory workers, schoolchildren, and housewives rushed to windows, mesmerized by the sight of the blazing freighter as it drifted steadily toward Pier 6.

While most people were watching the action in the harbour, Charles Duggan Jr. hurried down to the dock, where his launch was moored. He had witnessed the collision from the living room window of his parents' house, and was on his way to offer assistance. Like his father, Charles was a ferry pilot. Having grown up on the harbour, he felt more at home on water than on land. And, like most mariners, he was always prepared to risk his own safety to come to the aid of others. He hopped aboard his launch and started the engine.

Once he was clear of the wharf, Charles pointed the launch in the direction of the *Mont Blanc* and opened the throttle. Just as he was setting out, he saw the crew of the burning ship begin to spill over the side "like rats," into the waiting lifeboats. He noticed they wasted no time rowing away from the scene, but didn't give it much thought. Concerned that there might still be crew aboard, he continued moving toward the ship. When he was close enough to "feel the heat of the fire" on his face, Charles cut the engine.

Fred Longland had just arrived in Halifax that morning. Longland, an officer with the Royal Canadian Navy, was reporting for duty on the HMCS *Niobe*. Since it was no longer seaworthy, the *Niobe* was permanently moored at the dockyards. There, it served as a training and depot vessel. After reporting to the drafting officer onboard, Longland made his way up top. The manoeuvrings of the *Mont Blanc* and *Imo* caught his eye and he paused to watch. The frantic exchange of whistle blasts indicated trouble. Longland felt a pang of horror as he realized the two ships were on a collision course.

The Halifax Explosion

When the collision occurred and fire broke out, Longland hurried up to the *Niobe's* forecastle deck to see what would happen next. Word quickly spread that a ship was on fire in the harbour and the *Niobe* was dispatching a crew in the steam pinnace to help fight the fire. Before long, the forecastle deck was packed with curious sailors, all jostling for a good view of the action.

Meanwhile, Captain Brannen gave his crew orders to turn the *Stella Maris* back to the dry dock so they could drop off the scows before heading toward the burning ship to offer assistance. Horatio Brannen knew the procedure; he had been in the salvage business for nearly two decades. At 44 years of age, he was well known and widely respected for the many daring rescue operations he had conducted over the years. As the tug approached the burning freighter, Brannen ordered his first mate to break out the hose and prepare to fight the blaze.

At the same time, Captain Garnett of the British cruiser, HMS *Highflyer*, watched the action from the bridge of his ship. Captain Garnett, like most others in the harbour that day, was unaware of the deadly cargo in the *Mont Blanc's* hold. But he knew that a burning ship in such close proximity was a hazard, no matter what its cargo. Many ships in the vicinity had munitions on board, and fire and explosives were a lethal mix.

The Red Flag

Deciding something had to be done about the fire, Captain Garnett summoned his first officer, Commander Tom Triggs, to the bridge. Garnett ordered Triggs to send an officer over to the burning freighter to assess the situation. Triggs, feeling it was his duty, volunteered to go himself. Garnett approved, and within minutes, Triggs and a crew of six set off in *Highflyer*'s whaler.

By this time, a considerable crowd had gathered outside Uphams General Store on Barrington Street. Uphams overlooked the Narrows and offered a perfect view of the spectacle. The owner of the store saw that the burning ship was drifting dangerously close to Pier 6. Foreseeing a catastrophe onshore, he rushed inside to call the fire department. Before long, the clanging of bells echoed across the city as fire engines sped to the scene.

Unfortunately, the nature of the *Mont Blanc*'s cargo had been deliberately concealed. Flying a red flag signifies that a ship is carrying explosives. However, the *Mont Blanc* had not hoisted the red flag before entering the harbour that morning. It was widely believed that enemy spies were about. So, for reasons of security, Le Medec decided it was best to keep his ship's contents confidential. Consequently, few in the city were aware of the immense threat the burning ship posed.

One of the few privy to this information was

The Halifax Explosion

Commander James Murray, Transport Officer Liaison between the Port Convoy Office and the merchant ships. When the collision occurred, Murray was aboard a tug, returning from the Bedford Basin. As soon as his tug entered the Narrows, the commander caught sight of the burning *Mont Blanc.* He hurriedly swung the tug into Pier 9, desperately hoping to reach his office and send out a general alarm before it was too late. As the vessel met the pier, he leaped to the wharf and raced toward his office. On the way, he ran into a sailor. Murray ordered him to warn everyone in the vicinity that the burning ship was loaded with munitions and about to blow.

The *Mont Blanc* was now perilously close to Pier 6. To make matters worse, the railway yardmaster's building sat a little less than 200 meters away from the pier. Inside, dispatcher Vincent Coleman and chief clerk William Lovette watched anxiously as the burning ship drifted closer and closer. The fire posed a serious threat to the yardmaster's building, as well as the dozens of freight cars standing in the yards. When the ship slammed into the jetty, the two men grew alarmed. Within minutes, fire spilled from the deck onto the pier, igniting the wooden pilings and nearby sheds.

By this time, the *Stella Maris* was positioned alongside the blazing *Mont Blanc.* Captain Brannen and his crew were valiantly attempting to extinguish the raging inferno when Commander Triggs and his crew from the *Highflyer* arrived on the scene. Triggs could see that trying to fight the blaze with one hose was hopeless. He boarded the *Stella Maris* to discuss the situation with Brannen. After a brief conference, they decided the best course of action would be to attach a line to the *Mont Blanc* and tow her away from the pier. Out in mid-channel, they reasoned, she would pose less of a threat. This strategy would also allow other tugs to get close enough to help extinguish the fire. At this point, *Niobe's* steam pinnace had arrived on the scene to offer assistance.

Confident that Captain Brannen could handle the situation, Triggs left the scene and set off in the direction of the *Imo* to assess its damage. After the crushing impact, the Norwegian steamer had drifted into mid-channel, where it now lay motionless.

While Captain Brannen and Commander Triggs struggled to get the situation in the harbour under control, Francis Mackey and the crew of the *Mont Blanc* rowed furiously toward the Dartmouth shore. At the small settlement of Tuft's Cove, a group had gathered on the beach to watch the burning ship. As the French sailors clambered out of the lifeboats, they desperately tried to warn the spectators to run for cover. "*Courir! Courir!*" they shouted, gesturing wildly toward the burning ship and then to the woods. The spectators, unable to understand French, just stared at them. Finally, in desperation, one sailor snatched a baby from a woman's arms and sprinted off into the woods. The mother, nearby spectators, and the rest of the crew followed close on his heels.

Charles Duggan, the ferry pilot, watched the blazing *Mont Blanc* from his launch a few hundred metres away. He wanted to be sure there were no stragglers onboard before heading back to shore. When he saw the *Stella Maris* and the whaler from the British cruiser pull alongside, he figured the navy had the situation under control. Deciding to leave, he started up the launch and was just swinging around when he heard a series of explosions. He turned to see the barrels of benzol on the *Mont Blanc*'s deck lifting in the air and bursting into flames "with a roar." Sensing the danger of the situation, he opened up the throttle and sped toward the Dartmouth shore.

Meanwhile, in the railway yardmaster's office, Vincent Coleman and William Lovette were debating whether or not they should clear out when the sailor sent by Commander Murray appeared at the door. "That ship's loaded with explosives and about to blow!" he shouted, before disappearing as abruptly as he had appeared. The two men didn't think twice. They rushed out the door and across the tracks toward Barrington Street. After a few seconds, William sensed that the dispatcher was no longer behind him. He turned to see his friend running back toward the office. He hollered at Vincent, asking what he was doing. But the dispatcher just kept running, shouting over his shoulder something about the Number 10 Train being due at any minute, and that he needed to warn Rockingham to hold it up.

Chapter 5
Shock Waves

The apocalyptic blast ripped through the city with a force and fury beyond imagination. At about 9:06 a.m., 3121 tons of iron and steel exploded into millions of fragments, flying for miles in all directions. In the blink of an eye, the community of Richmond was laid waste; Halifax and Dartmouth were devastated. Houses collapsed, factories toppled, and churches crumbled. Ships, trains, and automobiles were hurled about like tinker toys. Roads were obliterated and railway tracks were torn from the earth. Trees and telephone poles snapped like matchsticks. A torrent of debris scattered everywhere. The blast shattered every window for miles around. Shards of glass ripped through flesh and lodged in eyeballs. Gas lines ruptured, and fire from hundreds of stoves spilled out onto the heaps of kindling created by the blast. Greasy black rain fell from the sky and shrapnel pelted down over the ruins for several minutes. The harbour became a seething cauldron. Its floor split open, propelling boulders up from the deep. And the force of the blast created a tidal wave, which swamped the shore. Small ships were swallowed and spit back out, and large vessels were ripped from their moorings and flung to shore.

When it was all over, at least 1900 people were dead, 9000 were injured, and hundreds were permanently blinded. Thousands of people were left homeless. And with electricity, gas, telephone and telegraph lines all severed, Halifax was completely crippled.

Charles Duggan was about halfway across the harbour when he looked back. The sight would be forever seared into his memory. The blazing ship "seemed to settle in the water. A lurid yellowish-green spurt of flame rose toward the heaven and drove ahead of it a cloud of smoke, which must have risen 200 feet in the air." Then came the most "appalling crash" he had ever heard. His launch seemed to be snatched from beneath his feet "as if some supernatural power had stolen her." He was plunged into the icy harbour, and "engulfed in a swirling, roaring mass of water," which drove him to the bottom "like a stone." After what seemed like an eternity, he surfaced — only to be caught up in a second raging wave. This time he was knocked unconscious.

The situation in the harbour was desperate. Thick black smoke hung over the water, ravaged ships drifted helplessly on the currents, and bodies and debris littered the water's surface. The *Stella Maris*, being closest to the *Mont Blanc*, had taken the full force of the blast. Amazingly, the little tug was not demolished, but blown downstream where it came to rest near the dry dock. She was stripped of her smokestack and spars, but still intact. Captain Horatio Brannen and 18 of his crew died instantly. Only five people onboard survived, including William Knickerson and Walter Brannen, who had been driven below deck by the blast.

Lieutenant Commander Tom Triggs was killed instantly, although a few of his crew in *Highflyer*'s whaler survived. The *Imo* was hurled onto the Dartmouth shore, her superstructure demolished. Captain Haakon From and pilot William Hayes were both dead.

The *Niobe* was also battered by the explosion. A hail of "boiler tubes, rivets and jagged steel plates" from the *Mont Blanc* had hammered the deck. The crew scrambled for cover as large chunks of plating flattened the ship's funnels. Men stuffed themselves into ventila-

The battered *Imo*

tor shafts, down stairwells, and beneath lifeboats to escape from the deadly storm of flying debris. When the tidal wave hit, the massive vessel was ripped from its moorings and heaved high into the air before being slammed back to the surface. When it was all over, the main deck was an "unholy mess." All four of the ship's funnels were demolished and its superstructure destroyed. In all, 19 men, including the crew of the steam pinnace, were dead. Dozens were severely wounded.

Almost every one of the 45 vessels in the harbour sustained serious damage and extensive casualties. The dockyards, Naval College, and several wharves were pulverized. Halifax Harbour, one of the busiest, most vital ports in the British Empire, was completely paralysed.

In Richmond, the students were in the midst of morning prayers at St. Joseph's School when the blast occurred. Seven-year-old Eleanor Coleman felt the building shudder and heard a tremendous crash. The Sister leading the prayers screamed something about the Germans attacking. The ceiling began to sag and crack, and chunks of plaster fell on the terrified girls. Eleanor's first thoughts were of her mother and her sisters, Babe and Nita, just down the street. If the Germans were attacking, what would happen to them?

The Sister managed to herd the girls out of the room just minutes before the ceiling completely collapsed. As they picked their way through the rubble, Eleanor heard moaning and crying coming from the other classrooms. The school was almost completely demolished. The explosion had ripped off most of the roof, and the floors had collapsed, one on the next, like

The ruins of St. Joseph's School after the blast

falling dominoes. The students in the Grade 8 classroom were stuck between floors near the top of the building. The stairs were gone, so the children had to climb out windows and jump to the ground to escape. One of the nuns was blinded by flying glass and had to lead her class out of the wreckage by feel. Miraculously, only two girls were killed, but many were seriously injured, including the nuns.

Once outside, Eleanor looked around for her brother Gerald, who had been serving in the morning mass at St. Joseph's Church next door. Not seeing him anywhere in the turmoil of the schoolyard, she started to make her way home. She couldn't believe her eyes. Where houses had stood along her route to school, there was now nothing but flaming piles of debris. All around her, people were running and screaming for help. Smoke stung her eyes and burned her throat. Eleanor could barely make her way through the wreckage. The Colemans' neighbour, an old man with a wooden leg, was crawling through the rubble. His wooden leg was missing. The sight of him dragging himself through the ruins of his home was pitiful. To the seven-year-old, it seemed as though the whole world had been transformed into the hellish abyss of fire and brimstone the nuns and priest were always talking about.

As Eleanor approached the spot where her house should have been, she began to panic. The house was gone. Like all the others along the street, it was now nothing more than a smouldering pile of rubble. Fearing for her mother and sisters, she started running. When she arrived at the site, Nita and Gerald were desperately digging through the piles of splintered boards and plaster. They could hear Babe crying somewhere in the wreckage, so they dug faster. The heat and smoke from the surrounding fires was becoming overwhelming. The children heaved boards and lifted sections of lathe and plaster walls that would have been impossible to budge under normal circumstances. Finally, they lifted away a portion of the kitchen wall to find their mother on the floor. She was unconscious. The baby lay half a metre from her, beneath the kitchen sink. Babe appeared to be unharmed, but their mother was in bad shape. With the fire drawing closer, Eleanor grabbed the baby, while Nita and Gerald lifted their mother from the wreckage. They decided to go back uphill toward the church, where they were certain they would find help. Russell Street was now an inferno and the children struggled through the wall of flames, up the steep slope to Gottingen Street.

It was about 9:30 a.m. before Frances Coleman regained consciousness. She was lying on the sidewalk on Gottingen Street. When she tried to move, a stab of pain knifed through her back. Nita and Gerald were hovering over her, their soot-smeared faces filled with worry. "Where's Babe?" she asked. "Is she all right?" Nita reassured her mother that the baby was fine. Frances was perplexed. The last thing she remembered was having coffee with her sister-in-law in the kitchen when they heard a "terrible crack." Her sister-in-law jumped up and cried, "Oh my God, the Germans are here!"

The Halifax Explosion

What on earth had happened? And why was she lying here on the cold sidewalk? Gerald explained that a ship had blown up in the harbour. Suddenly, Frances thought of her husband, Vincent. Was he okay? Another stab of pain shot through her. Everything went black again.

Jean Forrest had just finished helping her mother clear the table and was preparing to leave for work at the hospital when the explosion occurred. Her immediate thought was that a German fleet had slipped through the harbour's defences and the city was under siege. Jean, her mother and father, and the two plumbers who were working in the house, all scrambled for the cellar.

As a dedicated Red Cross worker, Jean had been prepared for an event such as this for some time. She followed the developments of the war closely. German U-boats had been advancing steadily over the past few months. It could only be a matter of time, she believed, before the war landed on their shores. After a period of quiet, Jean decided there was no point remaining in the dank, dark cellar without knowing for certain what had caused the blast. She left the others and went out into the streets. Seeing the cloud of smoke hovering over the North End of the city, she figured it must have been an explosion in the "magazine at the Citadel." She decided she'd better hurry over to Red Cross headquarters.

Meanwhile, at the Halifax County Academy, the students had just finished singing the morning hymn when the brick building "rocked and shook," and a "tremendous booming roar" was heard. Plaster and glass rained down around them. Evelyn Fox held onto the chair in front of her until the torrent died down. The thought crossed her mind that the Germans were shelling the school. Similar thoughts were shared by almost everyone in the city that morning. This wasn't too surprising. Only the week before, the headlines in a local paper read: "Toronto Startled by a Report that the Huns had Landed and that Halifax, St. John, and Ottawa were in Ruins and Quebec was Besieged!" The city had been on alert for such an attack for months. Now, it seemed, the assault had finally begun.

For several seconds after the blast, the entire assembly sat perfectly still, waiting for another strike. When nothing happened, the principal ushered everyone down the fire escape to the schoolyard. There, Evelyn was struck by the absolute silence of the city. It was as though the entire town was holding its breath. She had expected soldiers to be swarming through the streets, guns at the ready. The unnatural quiet chilled Evelyn more than the coolness of the morning air. Someone pointed to the smoke in the sky over the North

The scene of devastation

End and they all turned to see what looked like "a grey mushroom on a thick pallid stalk, silver-edged, black and purple lined, splendid but malignant, writhing evilly as it climbed and spread."

Dean John Llwyd was standing in the chapel of All Saint's Cathedral on Tower Road reading the Morning Prayer when he felt the earth tremble beneath his feet.

"A German shell!" he thought. He paused and looked up at the congregation. There were only three worshippers in the chapel that morning: his wife Marie, and two other women. A few seconds passed in complete silence. Llwyd cleared his throat and picked up where he'd left off in the Psalms. Suddenly, an earth-shattering roar drowned out his words. The stone building shuddered. Each of the large windows lining the north side of the building shattered in unison, showering a blizzard of glass down on the empty pews. The women gasped and shrieked. Llwyd felt his knees go weak. He feared the building was going to come tumbling down on them. In all his 56 years, he had never experienced anything so frightening. A feeling of utter powerlessness washed over him.

When the terrifying moment had passed, he ran to the doorway. The solid oak north doors, "which could have withstood a cannon shot," were ripped from their hinges. He looked out to see a cloud of yellowish-grey smoke rising high in the sky. As it curled and billowed higher and higher, it reminded him of "a huge flower unfolding in the air." Llwyd returned to his congregation. "It's all over, it must have been a munition explosion at some point north," he said. "We can go on and finish our service." But the women were clearly shaken. Marie's hat, he noticed, had been blown off her head and lay on the floor near the altar. After a few perfunctory prayers, he ended the service. The little group filed out into the bright sunshine.

After taking Marie home, Llwyd decided to head downtown to find out what had happened. He felt certain that there would be casualties requiring his assistance. At Spring Garden Road, Llwyd ran into a member of his congregation who had just come in on the train from Truro. Mr. Hewat told Llwyd that the explosion had actually lifted the train from the tracks. The man was obviously disturbed by the experience. He had been forced to disembark at some point before Richmond and walk through the devastated area. Now, he was pale and his voice quivered a little as he tried to describe the sights he'd seen in the North End. "Everywhere houses razed to the ground; buildings of considerable size, mere heaps of bricks. Fire has started and the wounded and dying are lying around in twos and threes."

Amazed by Hewat's story, Llwyd hurried over to the North End. He caught a ride with someone as far as the North Street Station, which stood on the edge of the devastated area. The station was an impressive Victorian-style stone building with a glass canopy covering the platforms and tracks. It looked as though it had been bombarded. The glass roof had come crashing down on the tracks. The battered cars were partially buried beneath splintered timbers and debris. And glass lay in glittering drifts everywhere.

Wellington Barracks, the large military compound situated just above the dockyards on Barrington Street, was also ravaged by the explosion. The compound housed the men's quarters, officers' quarters, married quarters, and the magazine, a small storage building containing munitions. At the time, the barracks was home to the 76th Regiment, a composite battalion whose main purpose was local guard duty.

That morning, as usual, the band played as the men marched into the parade square and lined up for inspection. Lieutenant Charles MacLennan and three friends stood at the north end of the officers' quarters where they had a good view of the fire in the harbour. MacLennan was a short, dark-haired man with blue eyes and sallow skin. Gregarious and excitable, he liked to be wherever the action was. Neither he nor his companions had ever seen such a spectacular fire. The three speculated about what caused the flames to shoot to the top of the tall column of black smoke. "Oil barrels vaporising," MacLennan suggested.

The next thing he knew, he was face down on the ground. He immediately jumped up and leaped into a nearby moat to find cover "before any steel arrived." For several minutes MacLennan lay there with his head down, listening to the shrapnel hitting the ground around him. When the barrage finally let up, he clambered out of the moat. He was unhurt, but a bit rattled. The garrison was in a state of chaos. The parade square, where only minutes before rows of perfectly groomed soldiers stood at attention, was now strewn with wounded men, broken rifles, backpacks, and chunks of debris. Among the injured was the orderly officer, whose thigh had been shattered by a piece of shrapnel.

Chapter 6
Beyond the Call of Duty

The first thing Deputy Mayor Henry Colwell noticed when he arrived at City Hall that morning were the hands of the clock tower. They were frozen at 9:06. The mayor happened to be out of town that day, so Colwell found himself thrust into the position of authority in the beleaguered city. And he faced every leader's worst nightmare. All communication with the outside world had been severed. The city's emergency infrastructure, unprepared for such a catastrophic event, had completely broken down. Half of the city was ablaze. The fire department had lost several of its firefighters, its fire chief was dead, and its only motorized vehicle had been destroyed. Although the city police force hadn't suffered the same kinds of losses, it was not equipped to deal with a disaster of this order. The hospitals were over-whelmed; a mass of casualties flooded into every medical facility and doctor's office across the city. Thousands of citizens were suddenly homeless and in need of food, shelter, clothing, and most of all, medical care. The situation was dire.

But if anyone was capable of dealing with such a disaster it was Henry Colwell. A born leader, Colwell was both industrious and resourceful. After taking stock of the situation, the deputy mayor got right to work. Rescue and relief were the two priorities of the day. The main requirement, he realized, was manpower. In Halifax at that time, the military was the only organiza-tion with the skills and manpower to contain the dam-age, help extinguish the fires, and rescue the injured. Since the phones were out, Colwell and the city clerk walked over to Colonel W. E. Thompson's office at the foot of Spring Garden Road and put in an official request for military aid. He requested assistance rescuing the injured, recovering the bodies of the dead, and fighting the fires. Colwell also made a request for items such as medical equipment and supplies, mattresses, blankets, and tents.

Colonel Thompson complied, and before long, the

military swung into action. Rescue parties were formed and began combing the ruins for victims and transporting them to hospitals. The disaster area was cordoned off with access restricted to rescue workers. In addition, a tent city was erected on the Commons to provide temporary shelter for the homeless.

Throughout the crisis, soldiers performed above and beyond the call of duty. They worked around the clock, often risking their own lives to rescue others. They distributed blankets and food to the victims, they gave up their beds, and many even gave the coats off their backs.

Deputy Mayor Colwell was assisted in his efforts to regain order in the devastated city by W. A. Duff, Assistant Chief Engineer of the Canadian Government Railways. By chance, Duff happened to be in town at the time of the explosion. When he discovered that all lines of communication had been severed and the trains were unable to enter the city, he quickly set out for Rockingham. His intent was to send a message to his general manager explaining the situation and requesting help. It took Duff a few tries before he managed to reach Rockingham, but once there, he was able to get through to the manager. The Canadian Government Railway responded immediately. Relief trains were organized to transport doctors, nurses, and medical supplies to the city. Within hours, aid began pouring in from all parts of Atlantic Canada and the Eastern United States.

Meanwhile, Charles Duggan regained consciousness onshore, coughing and shivering. He had no idea how long he had been unconscious, where he was, or how he got there. The last thing he remembered was watching the huge cloud of smoke rising from the burning ship as he sat in his launch, a few hundred metres away. He sat up and looked around. Eventually he realized that he was on the Dartmouth shore, near the French Cable Wharf. Almost directly across the harbour from his parents' home in Halifax. Up ahead, he saw what appeared to be the remains of his 36-foot boat cast ashore. Another, much larger, vessel was grounded a little farther down. It was tipped at an odd angle and looked badly damaged. In the distance, he heard screams and cries for help.

Feeling sick and dizzy, Charles struggled to his feet. He looked around in disbelief at the horrific sights surrounding him. Blackened corpses littered the beach. The harbour appeared surreal. Thick smoke hung over the water, and here and there black plumes spiralled upward. Smashed ships, ripped from their moorings, drifted among the layer of debris floating on the water's surface. The landscape onshore — a charred wilderness — was unrecognizable.

Staggering along in a stupor, Charles eventually came upon a general store. He opened the door, fell to the ground, and lost consciousness again. When he revived some time later, he was choking. The store was on fire. Unable to see a thing through the dense smoke, he crawled from the burning building.

Somehow, Charles made it to the South Ferry Landing. Oddly enough, the ferries were still operating. He boarded the first ferry that docked, intent on getting home. During the crossing, he overheard the other passengers discussing the explosion and the devastation of the North End of the city. He recalled leaving the house earlier that morning. His wife, Rita, with the baby in her arms, and his mother and father were all clustered around the front window watching the fire when he left. He prayed that the stories he'd overheard about Richmond being nothing but a funeral pyre were just exaggerations.

While Charles Duggan was trying to orient himself a few kilometres down shore, Captain Aimé Le Medec pulled himself to his feet and looked around. He couldn't believe he was still alive. The baby that one of his men had grabbed was wailing loudly. Everyone else was silent. Le Medec pulled a pack of cigarettes from his pocket and jammed one into his mouth. As he groped around in his pockets for a match, he remembered they had been banned aboard ship. His first officer was busy trying to round up the crew for a roll call. But several of the frightened men had scattered off into the woods the minute they were on their feet. After checking on all the men he could find, the first officer reported that it appeared only one man was seriously injured and in need of medical attention.

Chapter 7
Panic in the Streets

ith the orderly officer out of commission, Lieutenant Charles MacLennan assumed command of the regiment at Wellington Barracks. MacLennan had all those who were able — about 15 men out of 100 — fall in. The troop did a quick tour of the garrison, checking for fires and taking stock of the damage. Although the brick exteriors of the two-story buildings were strong enough to withstand the explosion, the interiors were in ruins. The roofs were smashed in, the windows shattered, and the walls looked as though they'd been hit with a wrecking ball. Stoves were knocked over and fires blazed throughout the complex.

During the inspection tour, Lieutenant MacLennan noticed that the garrison magazine was extensively damaged. The magazine was a small building surrounded by an iron fence. Situated in the corner of the compound closest to the harbour, it had been hammered in the blast. A 6.5-foot chunk of steel plating off the *Mont Blanc* had soared through the air and landed on the iron picket fence, leaving a gaping hole large enough for a person to squeeze through. The door of the building was blown in and the roof was partially torn off. MacLennan went inside to assess the situation. It was as black as midnight in the little building. He couldn't see a thing, but knew better than to light a match. Instead, he groped around in the darkness trying to determine the damage. The floor of the magazine was lined with wooden gratings. The gratings, he discovered, had been smashed into "kindling wood." The lieutenant thought it felt dangerously hot inside. Fearing the worst, he rushed out to get help.

After posting a guard around the magazine, MacLennan reported to the colonel, whom he found standing in front of his quarters. He informed the colonel that the magazine had been "shot to pieces." Unfortunately, the colonel's wife had been seriously injured in the blast. When MacLennan asked what should be done, the distraught man shouted, "To hell with the military magazine. My wife's bleeding to death! Get me a medical orderly." But there were no medical orderlies available.

MacLennan managed to round up a detail of about 20 men, and returned with them to the magazine. He set them to work clearing the flammable debris out of the building, while he went to check on the furnace room next door. What he discovered in that room was to trigger a wave of panic among the edgy citizens of the devastated city.

The little structure that housed the furnace had been badly shaken in the explosion. Coals had spilled out of the furnace onto the floor and had ignited. Now, flames licked the walls dangerously close to an open duct leading directly to the munitions storage area. Lieutenant MacLennan quickly grabbed a nearby fire extinguisher and began fighting the flames. He succeeded in dousing the fire. However, the smoke and steam billowing out through the hole in the roof and the open door was visible to all those in the area. The men working in the magazine were the first to notice the smoke. Thinking the building was on fire and the munitions about to explode, they ran for their lives.

Outside the garrison fence, a group of civilians noticed the commotion. The sight of soldiers and sailors fleeing from the burning building terrified them. Word that the magazine was about to blow spread through the city like wildfire. Mass hysteria ensued. Hordes of already traumatized people stampeded through the streets, heading toward the safety of open spaces. Many trapped and injured victims were left to die in the fires. Soldiers were dispatched to knock on doors and evacuate everyone in the city. Before long, Citadel Hill, the Commons, and Point Pleasant Park were filled with crowds of terrified souls waiting for the next blow to fall.

Unaware that his actions had caused such a stir, MacLennan looked out to see the men from his work detail scrambling to get through the hole in the fence. Instinctively, he dropped the extinguisher and began to follow. But the crowd trying to squeeze through the opening prevented him from getting out of the enclosure. He managed to get the attention of a man outside the fence and asked what all the panic was about. "The roof of the magazine is on fire!" the man replied. MacLennan paused for a moment to consider the situation. He realized that there was no point running. If the magazine were to blow up, he'd be killed anyway. Taking a deep breath, he climbed onto the roof to assess the situation. While it was damaged, there was no evidence of fire. Still not certain whether the magazine was on fire or not, the lieutenant decided to stick to his post and do whatever he could to avert a second explosion. A few of

MacLennan's recruits also held their ground. The men returned to the harrowing job of clearing out the magazine and hosing down the furnace room. Only after several hours of nerve-wracking labour was the danger allayed. Finally, people were allowed to return to their homes.

While the rest of the city was in turmoil over a possible second explosion, Frances Coleman was beginning to regain consciousness. Looking around, she found herself jammed into the back of an open wagon with several others. As the wagon lurched forward, each rut they hit sent a jolt of pain through her. She raised her head and looked around, trying to figure out where they were going. To one side was a large, open field, which she thought must be the Commons. She noticed a huge crowd was gathering in the field and wondered what was happening.

They finally pulled to a stop in front of Camp Hill Hospital. There, Frances was lifted from the wagon and carried inside on a stretcher. The stretcher-bearers set her down among hundreds of others and told her that someone would be along soon to take care of her. As Frances glanced around at the other casualties, the enormity of what had occurred began to take shape in her mind. Everywhere she looked there were bloodied, blackened bodies. The foyer was so full that the stretcher-bearers and nurses had to watch their steps. Sobs and moans filled the air. But the strangest thing of all was the number of people who were completely black, as though they had been working in a coal mine.

After the wagon departed with their mother onboard, the Coleman children weren't sure what to do. They couldn't go home; it was nothing but a burning pile of rubble. The school was in the same condition. They had no idea where their father was, nor did they know if their mother was going to survive her injuries. Thirteen-year old Nita saw that her younger brother and sister were looking to her for reassurance and direction. She decided that they should go to their Grandmother O'Toole's on Edward Street, in the South End of the city. Although she didn't voice it, she feared that their grandmother's house might be in the same state as their own.

When they finally reached their grandmother's house, Nita, Eleanor, and Gerald were relieved to see it still standing. Grandmother O'Toole, overjoyed at the sight of them, whisked them inside. She had been worried sick about her daughter and her grandchildren. After all, she'd heard rumours that Richmond had been completely wiped out in the blast. Since they hadn't contacted her, Mrs. O'Toole had begun to fear the worst.

While the Coleman children were being comforted and cared for by their grandmother, their uncle, Chris Coleman, was out searching the city for his brother Vincent, and his family.

When Jean Forrest arrived at Pier 2, she was astounded to find the hospital completely demolished. She was told to go over to the Technical College on Spring Garden Road. There, a temporary Red Cross headquarters and central medical supply depot were being set up. By this time, Jean had heard about the devastation in the North End; she was anxious to gather whatever medical supplies she could find and get over to the devastated area. She rushed to the college. The place was in a state of chaos. She managed, however, to find a bunch of bandages, dressings, and antiseptic, which she loaded into the Red Cross car. She intended to drive to the North End and set up a first-aid dressing station. Unfortunately, Jean had never learned to drive. So before she could proceed, she had to find a chauffeur. A co-worker resolved the problem by finding a man on the street who agreed to be her driver. Although she felt a little uncomfortable about being driven by a stranger, she quickly dismissed these qualms. Her main priority was getting into the devastated area to help the victims.

The Red Cross worker and her driver only made it

as far as North Street, where soldiers told them they weren't allowed into the area. Jean explained that she was a trained Red Cross worker there to help the victims. But the soldiers refused them entry, saying the area was restricted to all but firefighters and rescue workers. Frustrated, she asked the driver to take her back to the Red Cross headquarters.

Jean had just arrived back at the college when an officer came in and informed everyone that there was a fire in the magazine at Wellington Barracks. He ordered them to "get into the government field and lie flat." All the other Red Cross workers dropped what they were doing and headed for the Commons. But Jean was worried about her mother. She decided to go home and check on her.

While most people were desperately fleeing the North End in fear of a second explosion, Dean Llwyd was hurrying through the smoke and raging fires to the heart of the ravaged area. He had never seen anything so appalling. The entire area looked as though it had endured months of bombardment. The skeletal remains of a factory, a wall or two of a house, and the odd telephone pole were the only things still standing. Everything else was levelled. Bits and pieces of furniture stuck out from the piles of rubble, but for the most part, everything was smashed beyond recognition. Fires raged all around. Mangled, blackened bodies were everywhere. Smoke stung Llwyd's eyes, and the stench of burning flesh nauseated him. Nothing in his sheltered background had prepared him for this. He prayed for the strength to be of some assistance to those whose lives had been shattered that day.

Streams of walking wounded passed by. Blood flowed from gashes on heads and faces. Many groped along blindly. Some had limbs missing or dangling uselessly from sockets. All were in a state of shock. Several people shouted warnings at Llwyd about another explosion, telling him to get out of the area. But he continued on, stopping now and then to lend assistance. Eventually, he came upon a group of soldiers digging the wounded and dead out of the rubble. He stopped to help.

Noticing Dean Llwyd's clerical collar, the officer in charge came over and asked his advice about the disposal of the bodies. The minister suggested removing them from the ruins and laying them out for identification and pickup. Before long, the rescuers had more than 30 bodies lined up on the side of the road. Llwyd was astonished by the many different causes of death resulting from the explosion. Many of the victims had been decapitated — their heads and shoulders blown clean off, leaving only torsos and limbs. Others had limbs torn off, skulls bashed in, and great gashes in the torsos. One remarkable phenomenon was the number of deceased who had been stripped naked, but didn't have a mark on their bodies. Llwyd grieved for them all.

The men occasionally heard moaning, sobbing, and cries for help coming from the wreckage while they worked. Every now and then, the shrill whinnying of horses in distress came within earshot. At first, they assumed the sounds were made by the many spooked horses charging through the streets. But eventually the whinnying grew more insistent. Finally, the officer in charge sent one of the soldiers off to investigate. The soldier returned shortly, looking distraught. He had discovered a stable full of terrified horses trapped in the ruins, fires closing in all around them. Unable to free the horses himself, he'd come back for help. Disturbed by the news, several of the men stopped what they were doing and were about to rush off and rescue the horses. But the officer reasoned that it was more important to save human lives than those of animals. He picked a couple of soldiers to go help free the animals, and ordered the rest back to work. Soon, the disturbing sounds ceased. The men returned triumphantly, reporting that all the horses had been saved. This small victory among all the calamity of the day bolstered the men's spirits. They returned to their dismal task with renewed vigour.

Shortly after the explosion occurred, casualties began pouring into Dr. G. A. MacIntosh's home on Robie Street. The doctor, however, was on call at the hospital that morning. His wife, Clara, was still in her housecoat when the doorbell started ringing. She had been in bed when the blast shook the house. Although her bed had been sprayed with flying glass when the windows had shattered, the petite blonde was unhurt. But when she heard the maid screaming downstairs, she ran down in her bare feet to see what had happened. On the way, she stepped on the broken glass, lacerating her feet. Once the casualties started flowing in, however, Clara forgot all about her own injuries.

Clara MacIntosh was head of the Lady's Division of the St. John's Ambulance Brigade in Halifax. A high-strung, energetic woman with a gift for organization, Clara was undaunted by the overwhelming task that lay before her.

Many of the victims who showed up at the MacIntosh home that morning were neighbours or patients of the doctor, but a few were from the North End. One woman had walked all the way from the centre of the devastated area. She was a shocking sight. Her skin, hair, and clothes were completely black, and her coat was in tatters. She told Clara that she had been on the third floor of a house near the foot of Kaye Street when the explosion had occurred. The next thing she knew, she was lying in the street. She found herself completely drenched in a black oily substance, a telegraph pole across her chest pinning her to the ground. The woman didn't appear to be badly hurt, so Clara took her upstairs and ran her a bath. When the woman began removing her clothes, the doctor's wife was shocked by the state of her underwear. Like the rest of her garments, they too were completely black. Clara asked the maid to wash the articles, but the greasy substance wouldn't come out.

After the woman was cleaned up and given a cup of tea, she was put to work sweeping up the glass and plaster covering the floors. Several of the men had already been put to work. They boarded up the windows while Clara and the maid attended to the other patients, bathing and dressing their wounds and making them comfortable until the doctor arrived. By the time Dr. MacIntosh showed up at 9:45, the house was overflowing with casualties. They perched in the stairwell and spilled out into the kitchen, dining, and living rooms. Even the furnace room was packed with victims seeking medical attention.

Shortly after 10:00 a.m., a soldier pounded on the door and briskly informed Clara that the magazine was on fire. They were given orders to evacuate the house. Clara tried to explain that the house was full of patients, many of whom couldn't be moved. But the soldier simply repeated the order and moved on to the next house. Fortunately, the open fields of the Commons were directly across the street. Still, many were unable to walk, and had to be carried the short distance. In order to make the patients more comfortable, Clara had the maid gather all the blankets and rugs in the house and spread them over of the cold ground. After all, who knew how long they would be out there?

When the order to evacuate was declared, the first thing Josephine Crichton and her sister Helen thought about was their housebound friend. They hurried over to Queen Street and found the elderly woman sitting in the middle of the street "in the chair she had been occupying every day for nine years." She was so bundled up that only her eyes, surrounded by soot-blackened skin, were visible. The woman was such an odd sight that she spooked every horse that came down the street. Eventually, Helen was forced to take each passing horse by the reins and walk it by the woman.

Once the danger of another explosion was quelled, Josephine and Helen took their friend inside and got her settled. Then they headed over to check on their aunt, who lived on North Street. They arrived to find their feisty 86-year-old aunt sitting outside. Although her house was still standing, it was a shambles. Their aunt had sustained a few minor cuts and bruises, but she was fine. The girls wanted to help her get the house back in order, but she wouldn't hear of it. She insisted there were others in greater need. "Don't stay here, we don't need you," she said. "We have our arms and legs. Go North! Go North!"

Heeding their aunt's advice, Josephine and Helen decided to go to Rockhead Hospital. On their way, they stopped at Logan's Drug Store to pick up whatever medical supplies they could find. The store was deserted. Its large, plate glass window was shattered and a thick crust of glass and plaster covered the floor. The shelves were knocked over and the merchandise was buried in the debris. The only useful items they managed to scrounge up were one roll of adhesive tape and a small bottle of antiseptic. The girls felt guilty for taking the items, but since there was no clerk on hand, what else could they do?

The sights on the streets were ghastly. But Josephine and Helen, both Dalhousie University undergrads, persevered. Along the way, they noticed a huge fire in the distance. They detoured to get a look at the inferno consuming the Cotton Factory.

Rockhead Hospital, situated on a bluff next to Rockhead Prison, overlooked the Bedford Basin and the Narrows. It had taken the full brunt of the blast. Although the reinforced concrete walls remained standing, the building was a wreck. The doors and windows were shattered, the roof partially collapsed, and the pipes busted. Fortunately, the 80 convalescent soldiers occupying the beds at the time were relatively unharmed. They, like their counterparts at Camp Hill Hospital, had given up their beds. Those who were able were busy performing nursing and orderly duties. By the time Josephine and Helen arrived, all of the beds from the upper floors had been moved down to the lower floors. There was barely enough room to squeeze between the rows. Like every other hospital in the city, Rockhead was crammed with patients. There were three or four children to a bed, and Josephine discovered a dozen wounded children lying on the floor of an office.

The sisters reported to the doctor in charge — there were only two doctors in the whole hospital — and were instructed to bathe and dress the minor wounds. They were also told to leave the badly injured alone as they were better "with the blood congealed." It was so cold in the roofless, windowless building that the girls kept their coats and hats on the entire time. The floors, centimetres deep in water in places, were a problem.

Neither of the girls wore boots, so they had to walk on their heels through the flooded areas in an effort to keep their shoes dry. From the time they arrived until the time they left the next afternoon, Josephine and Helen never stopped. They dressed wounds, assisted the doctors, and tried to keep the patients warm by bringing them hot cups of tea and warm bricks for the beds. The sisters were astonished at the selflessness of their patients. Everyone, it seemed, was far more concerned about the welfare of others than about themselves.

Chapter 8
Exodus

By about 11:00 a.m., some semblance of order had been restored on the *Niobe*, and Fred Longland was detailed to take a platoon out to search the streets and morgues for dead sailors. The navy uniforms, with their bell-bottomed trousers, were a distinguishing feature that aided in their search. Longland and his crew were told to watch for the bell-bottoms. Whenever they saw a pair, they were to dig out the body and lay it aside for pick up. It was a gruesome task. The carnage in the streets was horrendous — the morgue was just as bad. Here, soldiers were busy carrying in load after load of bodies, cleaning them up, and laying them out for identification. Sick at heart after hours of the grim search for fallen comrades, Longland returned to the *Niobe* for a badly needed drink in the wardroom.

Meanwhile, young author Evelyn Fox left the Halifax County Academy with her schoolmates, Patsy and Rose, who also travelled to the city by train every day. As the trio headed north, the girls began to realize their school wasn't the only building affected by the blast. All along Brunswick Street, windows had been smashed out and doors blown off their hinges. The people they met along the way seemed to be in a strange, "trance-like state." When the girls arrived at her father's school, Evelyn went in to talk to him. The Alexandra School, being farther to the north than the Academy, had sustained far more damage. The mayhem inside took Evelyn by surprise: "Shreds of green blinds flapped at paneless windows, or were strewn across the floor where broken desks lay upon their sides, and slashed books and papers (many impaled upon long glass stilettos) mingled with inches-deep plaster and glass."

When Evelyn came upon her father, he was busy bandaging a gash on a boy's hand. Her father's face was pinched and pale. But when he caught sight of her, the worried frown vanished. "Douglas is all right," he said. "He stopped here on his way back to barracks to report for special duty." Douglas was Evelyn's older brother, a soldier stationed at the Brunswick Street Barracks. Until her father brought it up, it hadn't occurred to her to be concerned about her family. Seeing the bewildered look on his daughter's face, Mr. Fox realized she had no idea what had occurred. "A munitions ship blew up in the narrows," he explained. Although this clarified things a bit for Evelyn, she still had not grasped of the enormity of the disaster.

Before leaving, Evelyn promised her father that she would wait for him at the train station. On their way out, the girls ran into Hazel, another friend from the Bedford community. The four girls left the school together and continued heading north. They noticed that the farther north they went, the worse the damage appeared to be. "On North Street the houses were completely shattered, barely standing and utterly deserted."

The normally busy street corner by the train station was all but deserted that day. A few horse-drawn carts loaded with refugees, and others transporting casualties to the hospital, passed the girls. But the quiet was broken when four soldiers came running down the street shouting, "Fire! Wellington Barracks Magazine is on fire! Move south. Into the open! Everybody south!" Evelyn's three friends started to run, but she remained where she was. When the girls realized she wasn't following them, they turned back. Evelyn was torn between obeying her father's order to wait for him at the train station and the military command to move south. After some persuasion, she decided to go with her friends.

Before long, the girls were perched among hundreds of others on the eastern slope of Citadel Hill. The crowd was strangely silent. They crouched on the grass, peering anxiously northward. Most people were dressed inadequately for the weather. Many wore nothing but a nightgown or pyjamas, their feet bare or shod in slippers. Evelyn was glad she had managed to retrieve her coat from the cloakroom before leaving the school. Although it was a bright, unusually mild day for December, it was still far too cold to be standing around outside without a coat.

The sight of pillars of black smoke over the north end of the city escalated the fear of yet another explosion among the jittery crowd. For those who had already suffered so much that day, the Citadel was too close to the danger. Many decided that the best thing to do was to move farther west, "away from the harbour's munition ships and possible enemies, away from the fort's magazines." Caught up in the adventure of it all, Evelyn completely forgot that she was supposed to meet her father by the train station. Instead, she and her friends fell in with the mass exodus.

Exodus

Like the refugees of a war-torn nation, the victims fled with whatever remained of their possessions. A column of horse-drawn carts, wagons, and automobiles loaded with shell-shocked families moved across the city and out St. Margaret's Bay Road.

After walking many kilometres, Evelyn and her friends decided they had gone far enough. They stopped at a field where clusters of people were crowded around small fires, trying to keep warm. A tall, thin soldier with a friendly face invited them to share his fire. He introduced himself as Laurence, and told them that he'd just returned from France. He had been wounded overseas and sent home to convalesce. Like the other convalescent soldiers at Camp Hill that day, Laurence had given up his bed to make room for those in more dire need. The girls asked him where he planned to sleep that night. Laurence told them not to worry, he was used to sleeping outdoors in his greatcoat. Evelyn was reminded of her older brother, Ashford, who was currently serving in France. The thought of her brother sleeping out on the cold, wet ground with nothing but his greatcoat to keep him warm was disturbing. Suddenly, the war seemed very real and uncomfortably close to home.

The explosion was heard from as far away as Prince Edward Island. But by 11:30 a.m., word of the disaster had not yet reached the sleepy little town of Kentville in the Annapolis Valley. There, Dr. Willis Moore was preparing to make a house call when he received an urgent message describing the situation in Halifax. He was informed that a special relief train carrying doctors, nurses, and supplies was preparing to leave for the city shortly, and he was requested to join them. Gathering all the instruments and supplies he could carry, Dr. Moore rushed down to the station. A number of doctors and nurses were already there, including Dr. G. E. DeWitt and his daughter, Nellie, who had just boarded.

At Windsor Junction, they stopped to take on more medical supplies. At this juncture, they met the night express from Saint John, known as the Number 10 Train. It had just come from Halifax. When the doctors and nurses saw the Number 10, they got their first hint of the catastrophe that awaited them down the line. With its windows shattered and a load of casualties aboard, the Number 10 looked as though it had just returned from the front lines.

The Number 10 Train had been late that morning. As it crept toward Rockingham, Andrew Cobb glanced out at the dozens of ships anchored in the Bedford Basin. It looked like another convoy was preparing to set sail. The sight of the vessels cast a shadow over the otherwise perfect morning. After three long years, it felt as though the war was going to drag on forever.

At 41 years of age, Andrew R. Cobb was already one of the most renowned architects in the Maritimes. Prior to the war, his career had been soaring; he had won several of the most prestigious contracts in Nova Scotia, and his building designs received rave reviews. Recently, however, the war had begun to put a damper on his career. True, Halifax was prospering because of the war, and the architect was kept busy designing houses for the city's wealthy merchants. But commissions for the types of buildings Cobb was interested in designing were beginning to dry up.

Suddenly, a terrible blast jolted Andrew Cobb out of his reverie. It felt as though a giant hand had smacked the train, tipping it up at a precarious angle before dropping it back to the tracks with a crash. Shrieks filled the air as the windows lining the car blew in simultaneously. Then everything grew still. Shaken and uncertain of the cause of the blast, the passengers sat there for several minutes before the train crept hesitantly toward the city.

Africville, the small African-Canadian community on the northern tip of the peninsula appeared undamaged. But by the time they reached a point just before Richmond, the tracks became impassable. As the train came to a full stop, it was swarmed by hundreds of wounded and desperate people begging for help. They looked frightful. Most were covered with the black, oily-looking substance that had fallen from the sky during the explosion. Their clothing was ragged and blood-soaked. Cobb noticed that several people were carrying their wounded in bloodied sheets. Others stumbled along with towels, pillows, or anything else they could find pressed against wounds to stop the flow of blood. Something had to be done to help the victims and the only option, it seemed, was to take them aboard.

The conductor decided to dump the baggage and mailbags to make room for as many of the victims as possible. The passengers mobilized at once. The men began unloading the baggage and lifting the wounded onto the train. The women raided the dining car and sleeping compartments for table linens and bedding, which they tore into strips for bandages. As there was no doctor onboard, Andrew Cobb volunteered to go in search of medical assistance. The other passengers remained and began patching up the wounds. Cobb hadn't gone far into the wasteland before he realized his search was futile and turned back.

By the time the architect returned to the train, a military doctor had come aboard and was working on the wounded. Since things were under control on the train, Cobb and six others decided to go out and start searching among the ruins for victims. The first structure they came across had four people trapped inside — a man and his wife, and another woman and her small son. The entire house had fallen on them, and the rescuers could hear the victims shrieking and sobbing beneath the rubble. They shouted out directions to the men, who worked feverishly to find them. The job was almost impossible. Large sections of roof and walls, too heavy for the men to lift, had to be torn apart before they could be removed. But the rescuers had nothing other than their bare hands to work with. To make matters worse, the house next door was on fire and four children were trapped inside. The children's parents and several others were working furiously to rescue them. But it was clear from the intensity of the fire, and the children's cries, that they were being burned alive. Andrew Cobb, the father of two young daughters, found the children's tortured cries for help unbearable.

Meanwhile, the conductor of the Number 10 Train was not sure what to do once he had the train loaded with casualties. Since he couldn't contact his superiors for instructions, he decided to turn back to Rockingham. There, he might be able to make contact. Once in Rockingham, it was decided that the conductor should take the train to Truro, where the patients would receive medical care.

The Halifax Explosion

Major Avery DeWitt, the military doctor aboard the Number 10, had come in from Camp Aldershot to attend a meeting that morning. Fortunately, he had brought his medical bag along. When DeWitt boarded the train, he found more than 200 critically wounded men, women, and children aboard — far more than one doctor could manage. Meeting the trainload of doctors and nurses at Windsor Junction seemed like a godsend to those aboard the Number 10. One doctor and nurse from the train bound for Halifax joined the train going to Truro, and both trains carried on their separate ways. During the journey to Truro, Major DeWitt worked at one end of the train, while the other doctor and nurse were stationed at the other end. Despite the cramped, preposterous conditions, DeWitt performed two successful eye operations along the way. And although three children died before they reached their destination, many lives were saved aboard the rolling hospital.

It was only when they arrived in Truro that Major DeWitt discovered that the doctor and nurse who had boarded at Windsor Junction were his father and sister.

After hours of backbreaking labour, Andrew Cobb and the rescue party finally managed to free the victims trapped in the ruins. The man wasn't hurt, but his wife was badly injured. She had severe lacerations to her face and one eye had been gouged out. The other woman and her son had only minor cuts and bruises, but all four were in shock. Once the family was freed, Cobb was physically exhausted and emotionally drained. He left the others and set out for his office on Barrington Street. Although the sun was still shining brightly, a thick layer of smoke shrouded the entire north end of the city. It seemed like dusk. Tangles of downed wires, poles, and debris made walking difficult, and the sight of corpses scattered everywhere was distressing, to say the least. Hoping to find sanctuary from the horrors, Cobb wandered into the North Street Station. Although the fussy, Victorian style of the building was not to the architect's taste, it dismayed him to see the station in such a calamitous state. The destruction was so extensive that he wondered how they would ever manage to repair it.

When the ferry with Charles Duggan aboard docked on the Halifax side of the harbour, he stepped outside. Only then did he realize that he was still soaking wet from being plunged into the harbour. Numb with cold, he stopped in at McCartney's Billiard Hall to warm up before continuing northward. When he reached North Street, he saw that soldiers had cordoned off the area. He begged them to let him in, explaining that his family were in the area. But they refused to let him enter.

After being turned away from the devastated area, Charles hurried to his sister's place on North Street, hoping she would have some news of their family. When he arrived, he discovered his sister was unharmed, but she had terrible news. The rest of the Duggan family, including Charles' wife Rita and son Warren, his mother and father, his brother, and two other sisters, had all been killed in the explosion. As he listened to the horrific news, Charles remembered the terrible screams and cries for help he had heard when he had first regained consciousness on the Dartmouth shore. He felt certain he'd never be able to get those anguished cries out of his head.

Chapter 9
Casualties and Compassion

B y 1:00 p.m., Dr. MacIntosh had returned to Camp Hill Hospital, leaving his wife Clara and the maid on the Commons with their charges. There seemed to be no end to the wounded pouring into Clara's first-aid field station. Many came in an "almost dying condition." Although Clara was trained in first aid and had seen many different types of injuries in her life, the variety and severity of the wounds caused by the explosion surprised her. One young woman was brought to her with her throat sliced open by flying glass. The girl was bleeding profusely, and Clara was afraid the patient would bleed to death before she could be bandaged and sent to the hospital. Another woman, a regular patient of Dr. MacIntosh, came to Clara with her left arm twisted at a very odd angle. At first, Clara thought the arm must be broken. But on examination, she discovered a large, jagged chunk of glass driven in under the skin, above the wrist and up toward the elbow. The glass was "standing on end," causing the arm to protrude in this unusual manner. Clara extracted the glass and bandaged the wound, and the arm returned to its normal position.

Finally, after they had been out on the Commons for hours, word spread that the threat of the magazine exploding had passed. They could return to the house. Clara and the maid packed up their patients and moved their field hospital back across the street. For the rest of the afternoon, and all through the night, a steady stream of patients continued to arrive at the door.

While Clara MacIntosh tended to the victims on the Commons, Jean Forrest was preparing, once again, to enter the devastated area and set up a first-aid dressing station. This time the Red Cross worker managed to find a returned soldier to be her driver. He suggested they get around the cordoned-off area by driving up North Street and down Robie, out past the Cotton Factory.

The large factory, which employed around 300 people, was now a "seething mass of flames." Many of its employees had been crushed to death by the heavy machinery, which had crashed through the ceilings from the upper floors. Others, pinned beneath beams and concrete, were burned to death in the fire. Many workers in other factories shared the same fate that day.

In the fields beyond the factory, Jean and her driver discovered hundreds of people, many of them seriously injured and in need of hospitalization. They loaded as many of the worst cases they could fit into the car and headed for the hospital. The streets were clogged with wagons, cars, and trucks ferrying patients to the hospitals. Downed electrical wires, glass, and debris made it difficult to manoeuvre and the going was slow. After dropping off the first load of patients, Jean and the soldier headed back for another. They continued taking load after load of victims to the hospital until the car's tires began to blow out from driving over glass and bits of metal. One by one, the tires went flat and then fell off. But Jean and her driver, intent on saving as many lives as possible, refused to let that stop them. Eventually, they were driving on the rims.

Among the last load of patients they delivered to Camp Hill was a little girl. The mother, unable to fit in the car with her daughter, was frantic. She knew her daughter had to get to the hospital, but she was terrified of losing her. She had heard of several mothers being separated from their children that day. She finally agreed to let her daughter go when Jean promised to come back and tell her which hospital her daughter was in and how she was doing.

The relief train carrying Dr. Moore and the others arrived at the outskirts of the city about 3:00 p.m. The crumpled tracks and mounds of debris prevented the train from going any farther. The doctors and nurses were forced to walk about one kilometre before being met by a fleet of cars, sent from City Hall to transport them to the hospitals. As they picked their way through the devastation, the horrific sights sickened Dr. Moore. "Blackened tree trunks … standing gaunt and spectral-like" over "rows of blackened and often half-naked and twisted bodies" reminded him of "Dante's Inferno." The extent of the ruins, especially along the waterfront, was astonishing. "The greenish grey of the water with its wreckage in the harbour and along the shore was particularly gloomy." It was an overwhelmingly depressing scene, and the doctors and nurses hurried through the area, anxious to begin helping the victims.

The sights that greeted them at Camp Hill Hospital, however, were in some ways much worse than the devastation in the streets. Camp Hill was a brand new facility, built to accommodate wounded soldiers returning from overseas. Although it had just opened a few months before, the bland, two-story building now looked as dilapidated as an abandoned warehouse in the heart of the ghetto. Blankets, tar paper, and boards covered the smashed out windows. Out front, a parade of cars, trucks, horses and wagons, wheelbarrows, and every kind of conveyance imaginable, came and went bearing load after load of wounded and dying.

Inside, the dark corridors and dimly lit wards were packed with victims; 1400 men, women, and children were crammed into a space designed to hold fewer than 250. Every square metre of space throughout the hospital was utilized. Mattresses lined the corridors. Casualties were crammed into offices. Even storage rooms were packed with patients. "Men, women, and children were literally packed into the wards like sardines in a box." The multitude of filthy, blood-soaked victims evoked pity in the elderly doctor's heart. He had never seen so many people in such desperate need. But the thing Dr. Moore found most disturbing was the tragic loss of vision and horrible disfiguration of so many faces.

Shown to a makeshift operating room, Dr. Moore began the onerous task of trying to mend the battered and broken bodies. One by one, they were carried into the operating room, faces sliced open, limbs ripped off, and eyeballs studded with glass. The lighting was so poor it was difficult for the doctor to see what he was doing most of the time. The lack of proper equipment and supplies only made his job more difficult. There was not near enough antiseptic or anaesthetic to go around; in many cases, operations were performed without either. When surgical thread ran out, wounds were stitched up with ordinary cotton thread.

After several hours of non-stop work, the strain of the job began to take its toll. When a volunteer nurse accidentally knocked a tray of valuable surgical instruments to the floor, Dr. Moore flew at her in a rage. Instantly regretting his temper, he apologized profusely, helped her pick up the instruments, and got back to work.

The patients, he noticed, were in a deep state of shock. "The nerve centres … seemed to be numbed, and while such a condition seemed to mitigate somewhat the horrors of acute suffering … it did not augur well for the future." He feared the trauma the victims had suffered would lead to a greater number of deaths and slower rate of recovery than under other conditions.

The greatest numbers of casualties that day were caused by flying glass. Hundreds of spectators that crowded around windows to get a look at the burning ship were blinded when the windows shattered. In addition to being blinded, many were horribly disfigured by the flying glass. Jugulars were severed. Noses, lips, and cheeks were lacerated or cut completely off. One woman's face was almost sliced off. It hung by a small hinge of skin, "like a trap-door ... the nasal and frontal bones were cut away and the base of the brain was exposed. The wound was clotted with dirt and hair." Mercifully, the patient died before doctors could get to her. Still, there were others with wounds of this nature who miraculously survived.

At one point, Dr. Moore was asked to look at an urgent case that had just arrived. He was shown to an area where two female victims lay side by side on a bloody mattress. One of the women was already dead. Her half-naked body did not have a mark on it. The other was horribly mutilated "with one eye gone, the other apparently hopelessly injured, her face terribly cut and torn, blinded and disfigured for life." Yet the blind and mutilated woman had a strong pulse and was expected to live. The tragic irony of this situation was not lost on the doctor.

As doctors and nurses worked frantically to save lives, city officials struggled to establish order in the city. At 3:00 p.m., Deputy Mayor Colwell and the Lieutenant Governor met with other members of City Council to organize various committees and sub-committees to deal with the disaster. Six committees, including transportation, distribution of food and clothing, disposal of the dead, finance, and shelter for the homeless, were struck.

Housing was critical. Prior to the disaster, the city suffered from a serious housing shortage. And now, thousands more were on the streets. The committee decided that any undamaged public buildings, such as the theatre, the Academy of Music, and parish halls, would be converted into shelters. Organizations such as the Salvation Army and the Knights of Columbus, among others, immediately offered quarters for this purpose.

Blankets, cots, and bedding were rounded up from wherever they could be found. Partitions were hastily erected, and washroom facilities were improvised. By early evening, many of the shelters opened their doors and people began pouring in, grateful to have someplace to sleep that night. In addition to the public shelters, dozens of private homes took in as many refugees as they could manage. But despite these measures, many people remained on the streets, sleeping in doorways, abandoned buildings, and anywhere they could find a place to curl up.

After four straight hours of gruelling search and rescue work in the ruins of Richmond, Dean Llwyd needed a break. He asked the officer in charge if he might take a sergeant down to City Hall with him to make arrangements for the disposal of the bodies. At City Hall, he met with the deputy mayor and the newly formed mortuary committee. After a brief conference, the group decided that the Chebucto Road School's size and location — just outside the devastated area — made it the best place to set up a temporary mortuary.

With that issue settled, Llwyd went home to clean up before heading over to Camp Hill Hospital. The hours of difficult work had drained him, but as Dean of All Saints Cathedral, it was his duty to comfort the victims. Llwyd was much more in his element at Camp Hill than out in the ravaged streets. As a man of the cloth, he had spent a great deal of time in hospitals. Hospital visits were usually difficult, but rewarding. They allowed him contact with his parishioners, which he enjoyed. Today, however, the scene at the hospital was "heartrending." Llwyd felt certain that the sights he saw that afternoon would haunt him forever. Several victims were so badly mangled that it was difficult to discern age or sex. Many were bathed in blood, others soaked from the tidal wave or from being plunged into the harbour. With the windows out and the doors constantly opening as more patients were brought in, the hospital was extremely cold. The patients in wet clothing suffered terribly. Many died of exposure. Another troubling sight was that of parents wandering through the wards desperately searching for missing children, and severely wounded children crying out for their parents.

But in the midst of the mayhem and misery, the outpouring of generosity and goodwill warmed Llwyd's heart. He was awed by the efficiency and compassion of the battalion of volunteers and nurses who dressed wounds and tried to ease the patients' suffering. Many women who had lost their own homes and family members that day rushed to the aid of others. Hospital volunteers worked selflessly around the clock without complaint.

Llwyd overheard countless horror stories that were circulating throughout the hospital that day. There were several reports of naked women walking through the streets in a state of shock, having been stripped of their clothing in the explosion. One woman, it was said, had one of her breasts sliced completely off by flying glass. She was seen wandering through the streets in a daze, her amputated breast in her hands.

In addition to the horror stories, everyone was talking about the explosion. How had it happened? Who was responsible? Several of the casualties that had been on vessels in the harbour at the time told Llwyd their stories. Most claimed the French ship was at fault. One officer's description struck Llwyd as being particularly poetic. "It was as though the French ship burst asunder," the man said, "and showed a raging furnace within."

That afternoon, Evelyn Fox and her group of friends were standing around a fire in a field off St. Margaret's Bay Road when a young woman with a crying baby came along. The woman looked exhausted and dishevelled. Her dress was ripped and dirty, and her face smeared with soot. The girls offered to hold the baby while the woman rested by the fire. Assuming the young woman was the baby's mother, Hazel asked its name. "I haven't any idea," the woman replied. Seeing their shocked expressions, she explained how the baby had come to be in her possession. Her house had collapsed in the explosion, she said, but somehow she had managed to escape before it burned down. There had been complete chaos on the street. "All around people were running or trapped and screaming in the fires. I ran. Someone put this baby in my arms, I kept running."

The story astonished the girls. Evelyn noticed that the baby wasn't wearing any hat or coat. Its elaborately embroidered gown was bloodstained. Who were its parents? Were they frantically searching through smoking rubble for their child at that very moment? Or had they perished in the explosion? The thoughts were distressing.

After resting for a few minutes, the young woman rose to leave. Hazel went to hand the baby over to her, but she backed away. "I haven't anyone to turn to and nowhere to go," she said in a weary monotone. "The baby will be better off with you girls." Uncertain of how to respond, the girls simply watched in silence as the woman turned and tramped across the field toward the road.

Hungry and in need of changing, the infant howled constantly. The girls took turns trying to placate the baby. When Evelyn's turn came she held it close to her body, covering it with her coat. She could feel the tiny body stiffen and relax with the effort of its screams and wished there was something she could do to comfort it. After what seemed like hours, a young woman driving a cart arrived on the scene. On the back of the cart were a few meagre belongings and "several dirty, shivering children." The woman jumped down and shuffled over to the fire. She was oddly dressed, with a pair of men's rubber boots on her feet and a man's overcoat hanging from her narrow shoulders. The coat was unbuttoned, revealing a dirty rag of a dress beneath.

"I heard a baby crying," the woman said. The girls eagerly showed her the baby, explaining how they'd acquired it. They explained that the baby wouldn't stop crying. One glance told the woman that the infant was hungry. She informed the girls, "I'd better take it. I have relatives 10 miles [16 km] farther on, and if I can get that far, they'll have milk."

Relieved to be free of the baby, the girls handed it over. The woman tucked the baby beneath the bulky overcoat, climbed back onto the cart, gave the reins a snap, and plodded away.

Exhausted from the effort of trying to comfort the baby, Evelyn suddenly felt "cold, hungry and miles from home." She wondered where her father was and if he was worried about her.

While Evelyn Fox and her friends dealt with the abandoned baby, Captain Aimé Le Medec and his remaining crew were wandering around outside Dartmouth. The men were dazed and disoriented. They took turns carrying their critically wounded crewmember as they searched for a doctor. The ravaged landscape and hordes of dead and wounded they witnessed along the way were appalling. None of them could face the fact that they were in any way responsible for the disaster.

It was late in the afternoon by the time the captain and crew of the *Mont Blanc* stumbled upon a rescue party from the *Highflyer*. The officer in charge of the rescue party decided that the French mariners should be taken back to the *Highflyer*. There, they were held pending an investigation into the explosion.

By 4:00 p.m., the Red Cross car was completely out of commission. Jean Forrest and her driver abandoned it by the side of the road and looked around for another car they could commandeer. Every single vehicle in the city, however, was being used to ferry victims to hospitals. Jean couldn't bear the thought of the mother of the little girl they had taken to Camp Hill Hospital in the last load not knowing where her daughter was. She knew that if it had been her daughter, she'd be at her wit's end. Jean had promised the woman she would come back, and she was determined to keep that promise. Finding no alternative means of transportation, she walked all the way back to the fields beyond the Cotton Factory. By the time Jean arrived, dusk was closing in. She found the mother of the girl huddled by a fire with several other victims, trying to stay warm. The mother was overwhelmed with gratitude and relief to hear that her daughter was at Camp Hill and being looked after.

Some sailors were passing cake and bread around to the hungry crowd, but there was nothing for them to drink. Jean decided to look for some milk or juice to go with the bread. Since she hadn't noticed any stores

Rescuers sift through the wreckage at Richmond

along Robie Street — the route she and the soldier had
been driving along most of the day — she decided to
look toward Gottingen Street. She began walking down
Young Street. The only stores she saw were burnt out or
boarded up. She was stunned at the destruction in this
area. All day she had been on the outskirts of the devastated area, thinking that was as bad as it got. Now, she

realized that the situation was much worse than she had imagined.

After his stint in the ruins of Richmond, Fred Longland didn't have much time to enjoy his drink in the wardroom of the *Niobe.* Just as he sat down, a commander came looking for him. Someone at the Victoria General Hospital had asked for him, the commander said. Longland couldn't imagine who it could be since he had just arrived back in town. Still, he hurried over to the hospital to find out what it was about.

When Longland arrived at the Victoria General, he was shown to the bedside of a man who was completely unrecognizable. The man was "pitted all over with what looked like bits of cinder and was a nasty yellow colour." The patient was completely incoherent, and the only thing he had spoken was Fred's name. Baffled by the whole thing, Longland asked the staff to contact him if there was a change in the patient's condition, and returned to the *Niobe.*

It was three weeks before the unidentified man came out of his coma and Longland was contacted. When he arrived at the patient's bedside this time, he was surprised to see the mysterious person sitting up in bed looking quite normal. As it turned out, the stranger was actually a childhood friend of Longland's from

Waterloo. Oddly enough, the man had remembered hearing that Fred Longland was serving in Halifax. In his comatose state, Fred's was the only name he had uttered.

After the episode with the abandoned baby, the sense of adventure Evelyn Fox had felt earlier seemed to drain away. She now longed for the safety and comfort of home. Although Evelyn and her group hadn't heard whether it was safe to go back to the city, they decided to take the risk. The girls insisted Laurence, the soldier with the wounded foot, come home with them. At first Laurence refused, saying that he would be fine sleeping outside in his greatcoat. But the girls wouldn't hear of it. Finally, he gave in and trailed along after them. As the little group set out along the railway tracks heading for Fairview, the clear blue skies turned a dull, dirty grey.

By the time they reached Rockingham — six kilometres past the devastated North End — it was growing dark out. The glow of an idling train was the most welcome sight Evelyn had seen all day. Once aboard, she noticed the train wasn't filled with the usual commuters heading home to the suburbs after a day at work. Instead, the cars were crowded with the wounded and the homeless. Since the city hospitals and shelters were all overflowing, any victims who were able to make the trip were being transported elsewhere. This trainload was on its way to Truro and points beyond for shelter and medical treatment. Evelyn observed that, "Many of the faces had a bandage angling across the forehead, or holding a jaw; all were emptied and dulled by shock or grief."

The journey home was marked by tension and anxiety. The sisters who had invited Laurence to stay at their place had begun to worry. They wondered how their parents would react to them dragging home a soldier they had "picked up" during their travels that day. Embarrassed excuses and half-hearted invitations were lobbed around. Finally, Evelyn felt it was up to her to settle the matter. "I have a brother in France," she said. "If our house is still standing, there'll be room in it for a returned soldier."

Bedford, like Halifax, was immersed in total darkness by the time they arrived. The girls said their goodbyes at the station and went their separate ways. Laurence limped along behind Evelyn as she stumbled through the darkness toward home. She had not spent much time that day worrying about her own family. Now, she found herself filled with guilt and anxiety. Would the house still be standing? Would her father be out frantically searching the city for her? And what of her mother, brothers, and sister?

When they finally arrived home, Evelyn was almost afraid to go inside. The house was cloaked in darkness; it was impossible to tell if anyone was home. She took a deep breath and pushed the door open. As they stepped out of the cold into the cozy home, she was relieved to see her whole family sitting beneath the warm glow of lamplight in the kitchen. She introduced Laurence, explaining that he had given up his bed at Camp Hill Hospital and had nowhere to sleep that night. Without a moment's hesitation, Mr. Fox extended his hand to the soldier, took his greatcoat from him, and pulled another chair up to the table.

At 6:00 p.m., the temporary morgue in the basement of the Chebucto Road School opened its doors to those searching for missing family members. By that time, there was a long line of desperate people outside. Like many others that day, Chris Coleman had scoured every hospital and shelter in the city searching for his brother Vincent. He had found his sister-in-law, Frances, in Camp Hill Hospital earlier in the day. Chris promised her he would return with word of Vincent as soon as he could. Now, he waited in line with hundreds of others who had come here as a last resort. And like hundreds of others, he hoped he wouldn't find what he was looking for inside. When his turn came to enter the morgue,

Chris was filled with dread. He followed the soldier down into the cold, dimly lit basement, which was lined with row upon row of inert white-sheeted mounds.

Chapter 10
No End in Sight

fter stitching up casualties for hours, 62-year-old Dr. Moore was beyond exhaustion. In order for him to continue through the night, he would have to take a break. He was worried about his relatives in Dartmouth. He'd heard Dartmouth had been as devastated as Halifax by the explosion. But with the telephones out of commission, the only way Moore could contact his relatives was to go there in person.

A colleague who also had relatives across the harbour offered to go with Moore. There were no cars or taxis available, so the two men set out on foot. The streets were treacherous. It was impossible to see two steps ahead in the inky darkness. Even if the electricity and gas had been restored, the streets would still be dark due to the blackout order. This order had been in effect throughout Halifax for some time. Moore, in a foul mood, railed about the stupidity of the blackout order as he stumbled over the rutted cobblestones: "Every Hun officer probably is better acquainted with the harbour approaches than the pilots seem to be," he grumbled. "Yet we are in danger of serious injuries because of this puerile regulation while engaged in doing what little we can to mitigate the horrors of possibly the greatest catastrophe the world has ever known." His mood growing worse with every misstep, he continued to rant about the "appalling negligence, ignorance, and inefficiency of the so-called authorities ever known in the history of any port."

As the ferry churned across the dark harbour, the two men stood on deck staring back at the ravaged city. It looked otherworldly in the reddish-orange glow from the fires still raging in the North End.

Dr. Moore checked on his relatives and discovered that they had escaped with only minor injuries and property damage. Then he headed back across the harbour. Before leaving the hospital, he'd been asked to visit some victims in the North End who had not been taken to the hospital, but needed care. So, for the second time that day, the elderly doctor made his way through the ruins. By the time he arrived at the battered house, a snowstorm had begun. The victims he had come to see were huddled together in the dimly lit room. The carpets and boards nailed up over the windows and doorway were doing little to keep out the cold or the snow.

While Dr. Moore tended to the victims in the North End, the grief stricken Brannen family struggled to cope with the tragic events of the day. Captain Horatio Brannen's wife, Susie, had already been informed of her husband's death by the time her son Walter was brought home that evening. Walter was a dreadful sight. His face was bruised and bandaged. Since he had lost most of his clothes in the explosion, he was wrapped in a red tablecloth someone had thrown over him. He was in a deep state of shock. It was a miracle that he and William Knickerson had survived the explosion with only superficial wounds. These physical wounds would heal eventually; the emotional scars, however, would be with them forever.

Outside the magazine at Wellington Barracks, Lieutenant Charles MacLennan and his detail prepared to remain on duty throughout the night. Despite the fact that he was tired, hungry, and cold, MacLennan was determined to remain at his post. He and his men hadn't eaten a thing since breakfast early that morning. So, leaving one of the men in charge; he went in search of rations. Not far from the barracks, he discovered a bread cart that had overturned in the explosion, spilling its load onto the street. Grabbing as many loaves as he could carry, the lieutenant returned with bread for his hungry recruits.

When the blizzard began, MacLennan and his men erected a makeshift shelter from some poles and a few of the hides used to carry gunpowder found in the magazine. The temperature fell steadily until it was "perishing cold." The men huddled beneath the hides, stomping their feet and blowing on their hands throughout the long night.

For Clara MacIntosh, the night was promising to be a long one as well. At 8:00 p.m., she left her maid in charge of the patients in the house and went to check on the state of affairs at Camp Hill Hospital. When she arrived, she was shocked at the chaos that reigned throughout the hospital. It was almost impossible to get around without tripping over someone. The wounded, dead, and dying filled every nook and cranny. At one point,

Clara went to the kitchen to get a glass of milk for a patient only to discover "operations being performed on the kitchen tables." As she walked back through the ward, she passed a man lying on a mattress on the floor. He let out a terrible groan of pain as she passed. Clara checked on him and discovered that the man had a broken leg. His mattress was situated in such a way that everyone who passed by tripped over it, jarring the poor man's leg and sending him into a paroxysm of pain. She immediately asked someone to help her move the man to the only safe spot she could find — beneath a bed.

Throughout the day, Clara had been impressed by the fortitude of the victims. She could not imagine herself being as calm and courageous in such a situation. Many of the survivors had lost everything, including homes, possessions, and loved ones. Still, they didn't weep or make a fuss. Many were more concerned about the welfare of others than themselves. Several times when Clara brought a drink or hypodermic needle to a patient, she was told to give it to someone who needed it more.

By 11:30 p.m., Clara had been on her feet for close to 14 hours with barely a bite to eat. Suddenly, she felt faint. Seeing her slump against a wall, a nurse rushed over and caught her just as she was about to fall on top of a patient. Despite Clara's protests, the nurse ordered her to go home before they had to find a bed for her.

A bed would have been a welcome sight to Jean Forrest. She had left the North End and was returning to the Technical College to see what more she could do to help. Her legs and feet ached from the many kilometres she had walked that day. She longed to sit by a hot fire with a cup of tea, but she had to keep going. There were still so many people who needed help. How could she possibly worry about her own discomfort when thousands were in such urgent need? Jean arrived back at the Red Cross headquarters to find dozens of volunteers tearing sheets into strips and rolling them into bandages. There was none of the usual banter and laughter among the workers that night. Instead, a grim silence prevailed. Jean took her coat off and pitched in helping to roll bandages. Just as she was getting settled into the task, one of the supervisors took her aside and asked her to carry supplies around to the various hospitals.

Loaded with as many supplies as she could carry, Jean made her way through the dark streets. By that time, the cobblestone streets were covered with a slippery skim of snow. She slipped and stumbled several times, her load of bandages scattering over the snow. Finally, she arrived at the Victoria General Hospital, a two-story, red brick building in the South End. Although

there were several makeshift hospitals and dressing sta-
tions in operation all over the city, the Victoria General,
like all the other hospitals, was filled to capacity. People
were forced to wait outside. The sight of the victims
shivering in the cold as they waited for care was heart
wrenching. Jean said a silent prayer for them and carried on. There were still many hospitals to visit that
night.

Across town at Camp Hill Hospital, the sights and
sounds in the ward were unbearable for Frances
Coleman. She closed her eyes and tried to shut it all out.
Her brother-in-law, Chris Coleman, had been in earlier
and delivered the tragic news.

After searching all day for his brother, Chris had
finally found Vincent's remains at the morgue. The body
was burned beyond recognition. The only means of
identification were the watch and wallet found on the
remains.

The moment Frances saw Chris making his way
across the crowded ward, she knew the news was bad.
He told her that Vincent had died at his post, tapping
out a warning to incoming trains to stay clear. Vincent's
co-worker, William Lovette, had lived long enough to tell
the story of how the dispatcher had heroically sacrificed
his own life in an effort to save hundreds of others.

Frances was just 40 years old. She had already lost her father, a son, and now her husband — more loss than most people experience in an entire lifetime. She lay there in the hospital ward trying to sleep. But thoughts of Vincent, her children, and the tragic events of the day kept churning through her mind. It seemed the pain and sorrow of this day would never end.

12:00 a.m. December 7, 1917
The devastated city lay cloaked in blackness as rescue workers continued to comb the ruins for victims. The presses at the *Morning Chronicle* were busy churning out the next day's edition. The headline shouted: "HALIFAX IN RUINS." And below that:

Collision which occurred at 9:05 yesterday morning has laid the Northern End of the city in ruins. Mont Blanc a French munitions boat collides in the harbour with a Belgian relief ship and blows up. — Dead number hundreds and casualties are known to be in the thousands. — Every available place in the city being utilized as emergency morgues and hospitals — No cause yet found for the collision — Crowds of frenzied people rush through streets fleeing from what was first thought to be a German raid — Streets littered with dead — Practically two square miles of territory a burning ruin.

Meanwhile, the most ferocious blizzard to hit

No End in Sight

Halifax in years was gathering momentum, making the already difficult job of search and rescue almost impossible. While the fires continued to rage in the North End, snow swirled blindingly around Citadel Hill and drifted in mounds around the tent city on the Commons. In the harbour, battered ships were lashed by gale force winds. Crews cursed the bitter cold as they worked to secure the unmoored vessels. It was as though a supernatural power had unleashed a wrath of biblical proportions upon the city. Those whose houses were still standing tried to keep warm by the fire, as snow gusted in around hastily boarded up windows and doors. Few would sleep that night.

Epilogue

The Halifax Explosion of December 6, 1917 was the most devastating explosion caused by humans prior to Hiroshima. The repercussions of the disaster were momentous. More than 130 hectares of the city were laid waste. The exact number of deaths will never be known, but it is estimated that 2000 or more lives were lost. In addition, 9000 people were injured, and hundreds were permanently blinded. Of those who did survive, 20,000 found themselves homeless and destitute, facing a grim winter as they tried to rebuild their shattered lives.

For weeks after the explosion, the local newspapers ran columns pages long listing the dead, the missing, and those in hospitals. Eight days after the blast, the temporary morgue in the Chebucto Road School still held 350 unidentified bodies; soldiers were still digging bodies from the ruins; and family members were still desperately searching for missing loved ones. Dozens of infants and young children were orphaned. And many children were separated from their parents, some never to be reunited. Day after day, the newspapers were filled with postings describing children found, and others seeking missing persons.

Epilogue

The number of people blinded in the Explosion was staggering. It is estimated that between 200 and 600 lost their vision when windows all across the city shattered in the blast. In the days following the Explosion, hundreds of operations removing "hopelessly injured eyes" were performed. At the Victoria General Hospital alone, at least 60 operations of this kind were reported in a single day.

The Explosion physically and psychologically scarred many survivors for life. Months after the blast, deep psychological effects were only beginning to surface. Victims suffered complete nervous and mental collapse. Some, unable to come to terms with the horror and trauma they had experienced, committed suicide. Others lived in constant dread of another explosion. Loud noises or fire often triggered a panic response among the survivors.

As soon as word of the Explosion spread, aid began pouring in from all over the world. The American response, in particular, was overwhelmingly generous. Relief trains from Boston and New York carrying food, medical supplies and equipment, and hospital staff were organized and dispatched within hours of the blast. Many more relief trains followed. A Massachusetts–Halifax Relief Committee was established, and the outpouring of generosity from the people of that state was remarkable. Shiploads of glass, lumber, building supplies, clothing, blankets, food, and new trucks were sent to Halifax from Massachusetts. In addition, trade workers came to help rebuild the city, including dozens of carpenters, engineers, construction workers, glaziers, and plumbers. A plea for doctors and nurses brought hundreds from the East Coast to Halifax, including an entire medical team from Harvard University.

In addition to the outpouring of generosity from countries, states, and provinces, benevolent individuals and corporations also provided assistance. Sir John Eaton, president of T. Eaton Co., donated millions of dollars worth of medical supplies and equipment, clothing, building materials, and household goods. Not only did Eaton donate these goods, he delivered them in person and oversaw their distribution

Shortly after the disaster, the citizens of the devastated city began seeking answers and demanding justice. Who was to blame? How would they be punished for their crime? For those whose homes and families had been obliterated, the need for justice was great. An inquiry into the cause of the Explosion was set for December 12, but postponed until the following day. On December 13, 1917, Captain Aimé Le Medec took the stand.

Epilogue

In all, more than 20 witnesses testified, including crewmembers of the *Imo* and the *Mont Blanc*. Proceedings came to an end on January 28, 1918. On February 4, Justice Drysdale released the findings. A scapegoat was required, but Captain Haakon From and William Hayes were both dead. As a result, blame was placed squarely on the shoulders of the captain and pilot of the *Mont Blanc* and Commander Frederick Wyatt, the Chief Examining Officer for the port of Halifax. Wyatt was implicated, as he had been responsible for all movements of large vessels in the harbour.

Once Justice Drysdale's findings were released, Wyatt, Le Medec, and Francis Mackey were all placed under arrest and charged with manslaughter. Eventually, however, all charges were dropped. Aimé Le Medec continued serving as captain with the Compagnie Général Transatlantic for another four years. On his retirement from the merchant marine, Le Medec was awarded the Chevalier de la Légion d'Honneur. Francis Mackey, whose pilot's licence had been revoked during the proceedings, had his licence reinstated. He continued working as a harbour pilot. Commander Wyatt was simply transferred to another location.

Anti-German sentiment, rampant before the Explosion, reached a fevered pitch during the inquiry. In the minds of many citizens, there was no doubt that the enemy was to blame for the catastrophe. A vicious campaign flared up against anyone of German descent. Angry mobs attacked innocent Germans in the streets and vandalized their homes. Finally, all Germans living in the city were rounded up and placed under arrest. In such a climate of paranoia and distrust, enemy spies and plots of sabotage were suspected everywhere.

For the devastated city, the healing process began with a mass, multi-denominational funeral service for the 200 unidentified dead. Thousands participated in the moving service, which was held outside the Chebucto Road School on December 17. In the schoolyard, the mourners sang hymns and prayed as soldiers laid out the coffins one by one.

Bibliography

Armstrong, John Griffith. *The Halifax Explosion and the Royal Canadian Navy: Inquiry and Intrigue.* Vancouver: UBC Press, 2002.

Bird, Michael J. *The Town that Died: The True Story of the Greatest Man-Made Explosion Before Hiroshima.* Toronto: McGraw-Hill Ryerson Ltd., 1962.

Chapman, Harry. *Dartmouth's Day of Anguish.* Dartmouth: The Dartmouth Historical Society, 1992.

Erickson, Paul A. *Halifax's North End.* Hansport: Lancelot Press, 1986.

Kitz, Janet F. *Shattered City: The Halifax Explosion and the Road to Recovery.* Halifax: Nimbus Publishing, 1989.

MacLennan, Hugh. *Barometer Rising.* Toronto: McCelelland & Stewart Inc., 1989.

MacMechan, Archibald. "The Halifax Disaster" in *The Halifax Explosion: December 6, 1917.* Toronto: McGraw-Hill Ryerson Ltd., 1978.

Mahar, James and Rownea Mahar. *Too Many To Mourn: One Family's Tragedy in the Halifax Explosion.* Halifax: Nimbus, 1998.

Metson, Graham, ed. *The Halifax Explosion: December 6, 1917.* Toronto: McGraw-Hill Ryerson Ltd., 1978.

Monnon, Mary Anne. *Miracles and Mysteries: The Halifax Explosion December 6, 1917.* Hansport: Lancelot Press., 1977.

Richardson, Evelyn M. "The Halifax Explosion — 1917." *The Nova Scotia Historical Quarterly* Vol. 7 No. 4., 1977.

Ruffman, Alan and Colin D. Howell, eds. *Ground Zero: A Reassessment of the 1917 Explosion in Halifax Harbour.* Halifax: Nimbus Publishing and the Gorsebrook Research Institute, 1994.

Smith, S. K. *Heart Throbs of the Halifax Horror.* Halifax: Gerald E. Weir, 1918.

Acknowledgments

I am indebted to many people for their generous assistance in the creation of this book. Heartfelt thanks to Janette Snooks and Anne Finlayson for graciously sharing memories and information about their parents and grandparents, Vincent and Frances Coleman, and to Janette for the use of the photographs of Vincent and Frances; Jim Simpson for the insightful tour of the explosion sites; Dan Conlin, Curator of Maritime History at the Maritime Museum of the Atlantic, for his helpful advice and assistance; the staff at the Provincial Archives of Nova Scotia, and in particular, archivist Gary Shutlack for his assistance, advice, and insights; Alan Ruffman for his advice and suggestions; Douglas Shand for the biographical material on Evelyn Richardson; and Brian Cuthbertson, archivist at All Saints Cathedral, for the information on Dean Llwyd.

I am also deeply indebted to all the fine authors whose books and articles on the Explosion have provided me with facts, anecdotes, quotes, and general background material. In particular, Michael J. Bird's chronicle of the event in *The Town that Died; The Halifax Explosion: December 6, 1917*, edited by Graham Metson;

The Halifax Explosion

and *Shattered City: The Halifax Explosion and the Road to Recovery* by Janet Kitz.

The MacMechan collection of personal narratives, letters, journals, news clippings, and reports in PANS was an invaluable source of material. As were the "Explosion Papers," and the PANS on-line Explosion Remembrance Book. Evelyn M. Richardson's sumptuously detailed first-hand account: "The Halifax Explosion — 1917" published in *The Nova Scotia Historical Quarterly* provided a powerful impression of the event through the eyes of a teenager. The unpublished manuscripts of G. K. Brannen and Thelma Dasbourg on Captain Horatio Brannen in the Maritime Museum of the Atlantic provided insights and background into the life of Horatio Brannen.

Support and encouragement from many people sustained me through the various stages of this project. I am eternally grateful to Sandra Phinney for getting me started and keeping me going; Jane Buss at the Writers' Federation of Nova Scotia for generously sharing her wisdom and knowledge of all things literary; Nancy Cole, John Perry, and Mark Chatham for their careful reading of the manuscript, insightful suggestions for improvements, and constant encouragement; Kara Turner at Altitude Publishing for giving me the opportunity to tell this amazing story; and to my fine team of editors — Jill Foran and Jennifer Nault — who helped to shape and refine it. Finally, this book would not have been possible without the understanding, support, and constant encouragement of my husband, Doug, and my family.

About the Author

Joyce Glasner is a freelance writer in Halifax.

Photo Credits

Cover: National Archives of Canada; **Nova Scotia Archives:** pages 8, 43, 45, & 103; **National Archives of Canada:** page 50; **Janette Snooks:** pages 20 & 21.

OTHER AMAZING STORIES

These titles are available wherever you buy books. If you have trouble finding the book you want, call the Altitude order desk at 1-800-957-6888, e-mail your request to: orderdesk@altitudepublishing.com or visit our Web site at www.amazingstories.ca

All titles retail for $9.95 Cdn or $7.95 US. (Prices subject to change.)

New AMAZING STORIES titles are published every month. If you would like more information, e-mail your name and mailing address to: amazingstories@altitudepublishing.com.